ONE WORLD OR NONE:
PRESCRIPTION FOR SURVIVAL

ONE WORLD OR NONE: PRESCRIPTION FOR SURVIVAL

ERROL E. HARRIS

JX
1954
.H288
1993
West

HUMANITIES PRESS
NEW JERSEY

First published in 1993 by
Humanities Press International, Inc.,
165 First Avenue, Atlantic Highlands, New Jersey 07716

© 1993 by Errol E. Harris

Appendix © 1977 by the World Constitution and Parliament Association

The Appendix has been reprinted by permission of the
World Constitution and Parliament Association.

Library of Congress Cataloging-in-Publication Data
Harris, Errol E.
One world or none : prescription for survival / by Errol E. Harris.
p. cm.
Includes bibliographical references and index.
ISBN 0–391–03812–5 (clth)
ISBN 0–391–03801–X (pbk)
1. International organization. 2. International relations.
JX1954.H288 1993
341.2—dc20   92–33138
CIP

A catalog record for this book is available from the British Library

All rights reserved. No part of this publication may be
reproduced or transmitted, in any form or by any means,
without written permission from the publisher.

Printed in the United States of America

And he shall judge among many people, and rebuke strong nations afar off; and they shall beat their swords into ploughshares, and their spears into pruninghooks: nation shall not lift up a sword against nation, neither shall they learn war any more. But they shall sit every man under his vine and under his fig tree; and none shall make them afraid . . .

MICAH 4. 3–4

Contents

Contents

Preface

We usually consider ourselves to be the most intelligent animals on Earth, and some would say that we are the only ones. Certainly, no other species is capable of reflective thought, of taking stock of the situation in which its members find themselves and of the way they conduct themselves in it. Even when we blame ourselves or others for being stupid, it is only because we *are* intelligent animals that we can do so—we never accuse trees or snails of stupidity, and we only regard higher animals as stupid when we judge them by standards that we apply to ourselves. Being intelligent, then, if we find ourselves in unpleasant or dangerous circumstances, we commonly do something about it, and try to improve conditions, to protect ourselves against dangers, or to extricate ourselves from uncomfortable entanglements. At the present time, however, human beings are surrounded by the most horrific threats from several causes all the result of their own practices, in a man-made situation that is endangering the very survival of life on Earth. They are undoubtedly intelligent enough to do something to improve matters, yet nobody seems to be doing very much that is either adequate or sufficiently expeditious. What the reason for this perilous inertia may be I shall try to determine in what follows, as well as what courses of action can remedy it, and which cannot, and why they cannot.

The arguments that I shall present are not new. I have myself urged them twice before, once as long ago as 1950 and again fifteen years later; and other writers more influential than I have done likewise. But they are still widely ignored. The conclusion to which they cogently lead is commonly discounted, or even contemptuously dismissed out of hand. With mankind in so perilous a situation as at present, such obtuseness is not simply frightening, it is intolerable. That is why I am again trying to state and update what seems to me to be an unanswerable case for the only prudent and practicable course of action, and one urgently, or indeed desperately, necessary.

The argument is simple, obvious, and straightforward: (a) the Earth's environment is rapidly being disrupted with potentially disastrous effects on human and all other life; (b) prompt remedial action is imperative, but is not being taken; (c) no expedients can be satisfactorily effective unless they are global in scope, therefore none taken simply by national governments can be sufficient; (d) international agreements to act in concert are of little use unless their observance can be guaranteed, which, among national sovereign states, is impossible, because there are no means of enforcement (short of military action which defeats the object of the agreement); (e) consequently, it is essential to establish immediately a form of world authority that can legislate globally and enforce world law on individuals without resort to warfare. The purpose of the following chapters is to develop this argument in more detail.

The planet Earth is uniquely endowed with attributes that support life. No other planet in the solar system is like it in this respect, and the conditions indispensable for the generation, evolution, and sustenance of intelligent life are so interlinked and finely adjusted that the probability of their all occurring together anywhere at all is extremely low. No other planet known to us is provided so copiously with water, a very unusual compound with very special properties all especially favorable to life—in fact, living creatures are mostly composed of water, and for a large proportion of them it is the medium in which alone they can subsist. Almost certainly life originated in the seas and invaded the land only after millions of years of evolution. Moreover, water is the only liquid that is lighter in the solid than in the liquid state; so ice floats, leaving warmer water below in which living things can survive.

No other planet has an atmosphere consisting of just the right mixture of gases essential for the support of life. The most important of these gases are oxygen and carbon dioxide, and both oxygen and carbon have special properties distinguishing them from the elements closely related to them chemically. For instance, carbon dioxide (CO_2) is gaseous at those temperatures suitable for life, whereas the oxide of silicon, an element similar to carbon, is a rock-hard mineral. Only in the gaseous state can CO_2 be absorbed by plants, and its ready solubility in water makes it easily transferable from the air into living bodies, and from them again back into the air. A layer of ozone, a gas akin to oxygen (its molecules are composed of three oxygen atoms), protects the surface of the Earth from ultraviolet radiation from the Sun, which is lethal to living forms.

Moreover, oxygen is produced by plants in the course of photosynthesis, the use of the Sun's light to synthesize substances essential to all life, which animals (unable to photosynthesize) must obtain by eating plants. But chlorophyl, the chemical indispensable for photosynthesis, can absorb only light of a certain yellow color, which happens to be the color of sunlight, peculiar to stars of the mass and age of our Sun.

The Earth revolves around the Sun in an almost circular orbit, so that it is always virtually the same distance away from its source of light and heat. Its temperature, therefore, does not vary excessively between summer and winter. It rotates on its axis at just the right speed to prevent one hemisphere from heating up enormously while the other becomes exceedingly cold, as happens on the Moon. Its atmosphere, containing water vapor, moderates changes of temperature between night and day, as well as between the seasons; so too water vapor contributes to the greenhouse effect (the trapping of heat within the envelope of the atmosphere), produced by the presence of carbon dioxide and some other gases, maintaining an equable temperature throughout the year.

These are just a few examples of the extraordinary combination of conditions existing on this planet conducive to the maintenance of intelligent life such as our own. But today people all over the world are behaving in ways that are rapidly destroying this wonderfully harmonious convergence of physical and chemical characteristics of our planetary environment, threatening climatic catastrophe and profound changes inimical to life on Earth. The facts have been known for over two decades, but little, if anything significant, has been done, or is being done, to change people's behavior, or to improve matters. We must not and cannot allow this lethargy to continue. As we are rational beings, we should not behave like the Gadarene swine, rushing headlong, blindly, and mindlessly to our own destruction. That is why I am once again setting out to consider the current condition of mankind, to examine its underlying causes, to discover why they are not being removed, and to advocate what seems obviously to be the one feasible and effective way of devising a remedy.

My plea to the reader is that he or she will give careful thought to the arguments I advance, and will not simply dismiss them because they seem extreme or unusual (they are not exclusively mine, but have been set out by many learned and highly competent theorists). Consider the evidence, which is by no means scanty and is easily available. Watch the news broadcasts on television and read the daily papers, and you will find that almost every item of international news could serve as an example to illustrate some point made in the following pages. Consider the arguments I put forward and draw the clear and natural conclusion. If you do, I am confident that you will see that it is neither fantastic nor visionary, and that no other is realistic or practical. That being so, it immediately becomes apparent that it is imperative to follow it out in action, swiftly, vigorously, and determinedly. Any risks that it may involve are infinitely less than those presented by the one inevitable alternative. And the action called for is nothing remote or beyond what each and all of us can immediately embark upon. Once persuaded, we can but go resolutely forward.

The readers to whom I am appealing are ordinary people, not only academics and professionals, but also the intelligent majority without special learning. I have not, therefore, burdened the text with footnotes and learned references, which might only distract from the main argument. If any wish to consult the experts in legal and political theory, or in ecological sciences, I have provided a bibliography which should be a guide to such further instruction as may be desired. Most of the facts to which I am appealing are pretty well known, and many can be discovered from reading the daily newspapers. What I am asking the reader to do is to consider the implications of these facts, and to put two and two together. To my mind, they lead to an inescapable conclusion, which clearly calls for obvious and immediate action on the part of all citizens who have eyes to see and ears to hear, who can recognize the extremity of the dangers by which the whole of humanity is beset, and the one and only way to avert them.

The means of survival are already provided, they are virtually in our hands; all we need do is to grasp them and put them to use. They are the only means, as the argument in the following chapters seeks to establish; yet few people seem to recognize that this is the case; few are willing to embrace the one and only method of escape from the predicament in which mankind is now placed. We are blinkered by habits of thought and practice, which themselves are the main causes of the dangers we have created, and are continuing to create, for ourselves. It is time, almost past time, that we awoke to the realities of the situation and took determined action to set matters to rights.

So let us begin by reviewing the state of the planet and continue by taking stock of the international situation. Let us then consider the various suggestions that have been made for extricating the human race from its self-made emergency to see whether and how far they may be practicable. We should then be able to see the right way forward, and to realize that if we ignore it, or procrastinate, we do so at our utmost peril.

1

The State
of the Planet

As we approach the end of the twentieth century A.D., humankind is
threatened with extinction from numerous angles. Scientists have established the fact that the Earth is a single system maintaining itself as a
congenial habitat for life in the plenteous energy flow from the Sun; but the
activities and the life-style of mankind is now disrupting the environment
and destroying the ecology that sustains life, its own along with all other.
This insidious depletion of the biosphere results from deliberate, as well
as inadvertent, human behavior; but, as human beings are intelligent
animals, once they have been apprised of the menacing facts, they should
be able to seek ways of countering the impending dangers, and, it is to be
hoped, to find effective remedies. Until now, however, in spite of authoritative scientific reports, no very reassuring measures have been taken to
stem the deterioration, the scale of which, as we shall presently discover,
is truly daunting.

Since 1945, the continued existence of human civilization, and more
recently of human life itself, has been put in jeopardy by the imminent
possibility of war, in which the use of nuclear weapons would wipe out
living beings, not only by their immediate destructive power, but also
through the resultant radioactive fallout, and pollution of the upper atmosphere, that would reduce the global temperature and inaugurate a new and
severe ice age (the so-called nuclear winter), which few if any species could
survive. If that threat has temporarily receded, it has not been eliminated, as
we shall later see reason to admit. But, meanwhile, new menaces have
arisen, from destructive causes operating in almost every quarter of the

1

globe, the mitigation and removal of which, if it is possible, presents mankind with the most pressing and the most egregious problems. The purpose of what follows is to set out what the most urgent of these problems are and to consider what action is essential if they are to be met. Let us begin by reviewing the state of the planet at the present time.

POPULATION

The present population of the world is 5.2 billion, virtually double what it was at the beginning of this century, and it is increasing at the rate of approximately 1 billion (roughly the population of Mexico) every decade. If this rate of increase continues world population will reach 8.5 billion by the year 2025 and will grow to about 16 billion by the end of the next century. It is quite clear, and is generally agreed by the experts, that this rate of growth cannot be sustained because the resources of the Earth cannot supply the vital needs of so enormous a population.

Whenever the numbers of a species increase so as to exceed the sustenance that the environment can provide, either it tends to die back through lack of provender, or is reduced by predation, or both; or in its search for food it may self-destruct, like the lemmings of Norway which run until they reach the seashore and then swim out to sea until they drown. In one or the other of these ways the balance of nature is restored. But when the species is human its members take deliberate steps to overcome the shortage of provisions, their medical science helps them to reduce the ravages of disease, and other conscious efforts to keep the race alive are adopted. At the present time, however, these deliberate measures are having effects contrary to those intended; they are depleting natural resources and disrupting the ecology in ways that endanger the survival of mankind along with the other species on which that survival depends.

More people need more food, the main sources of which for human beings are agriculture and fisheries. They need more housing and shelter, and, as the countryside offers less means of living and insufficient work, they tend to congregate more and more in the cities. They need more clothing, furniture, appliances, and countless other amenities, which swell the demand for manufacture and industry, which require energy, light, and heat, which intensify the need for yet more energy; they seek recreation, which among other effects, increases the appeal of tourism. All these demands, at the present time, are creating environmental strains, polluting water and air, depleting the soil, destroying the forests, and endangering other species along with our own, and in numerous ways threatening the survival of the very people they are intended to sustain. The effects are not simply additive, but mutually interactive and exacerbating. Let us consider each of the most significant factors in turn, beginning with the supply of food.

AGRICULTURE

Already in the earlier decades of this century the means of feeding so rapidly increasing a population had become a world problem of major dimensions; but then, in the 1960s, there occurred what has come to be called the green revolution. The generation by biologists of new varieties of grain giving increased yield, the use of mineral fertilizers and chemical pesticides, and the implementation of new methods of land management expanded agricultural production to such an extent that, even despite the burgeoning population figures, consumption per capita was increased during the 1970s and later. But since 1984 the world production of grain has ceased to keep pace with population growth, new ways of repeating the green revolution have not been available, and its more sinister effects have begun to take their toll. Conditions for agricultural production have seriously deteriorated, and we are now faced with global problems of immense proportions.

Recent studies have shown that the world has lost one-fifth of its arable land in the past decade (an area equal to China and India combined) through causes such as erosion, overintensive cultivation, poor irrigation practices, deforestation, desertification, and urbanization.

Grain production always tends to concentrate on the growth of a few high-yield species, but the effect of the green revolution has been to confine this concentration to the new varieties that biologists have more or less invented by hybridization and selection, if not by biological engineering. The result has been and increasingly is the loss of natural species better adapted to local environments, which would have been more appropriate to local needs, and on which agriculturists might have relied as reserves when conditions deteriorate so as to make those strains in use less satisfactory. As we shall later observe, the loss of species is itself a lamentable feature of current environmental deterioration, with direct and indirect effects on the chances of human survival.

New methods of land management encouraged by the need to increase crop production have enlarged the size of fields and have led to the aban-donment of traditional practices, such as the rotation of crops, and alternate crop raising on small allotments. Farmers have been induced not only to omit rotation, but also to cultivate continuously fields formerly left fallow in alternate years. Where contour ploughing was needed to conserve the topsoil, it has now been discontinued. This, as well as the extension of cultivation to less fertile areas with the help of artificial fertilizers, has exacerbated erosion of the soil and hastened its exhaustion. The U.S. Department of Agriculture estimated in 1980 that nearly 2.8 billion tons of topsoil (6.8 tons per acre) was lost to wind and water erosion per annum in the United States; estimates for what was formerly the Soviet Union are at least as great; for India they show the situation there to be twice as bad, and even worse in China.[1] Al Gore records that Iowa once had an average of sixteen feet of topsoil on its surface, but today only half that depth is left, the rest having been carried away to the Mississippi and the sea.[2] The felling of woodland windbreaks and the grubbing up of hedgerows to enlarge ploughlands for modern farming have increased wind erosion in the drier areas and have further destroyed the habitats of numerous species of birds and small mammals. In Britain the corncrake and the nightjar are only two of the many species of birds that have become well-nigh extinct as a result of the contemporary revolution in farming methods.

Natural manures and vegetable composts enrich the soil, but mineral fertilizers required by contemporary intensive cultivation tend to impoverish it. Even worse, they are washed out into the rivers and lakes and pollute waters that then become uninhabitable by the fish and aquatic mammals that normally live in them. Many species of waterfowl and waders thus lose their source of food and either migrate or die off; and water needed for human consumption and other uses is poisoned. As we read in *State of the World—1992*:

> Chemical runoff and soil erosion from farms on the Belize coast . . . constitute one of the greatest threats to that nation's barrier reef; aquatic ecosystems in the United States and Europe suffer acutely from pollution from croplands. In the United Kingdom, many bird species have declined over the past 20–30 years, likely due to herbicide use and the elimination of hedgerows and unused lands from agricultural landscapes.[3]

Nitrogen and phosphorus in fertilizers increase the growth of algae in streams, estuaries, and lakes, which use up the oxygen supply and choke out vegetable life, starve the fish, and decimate the waterfowl.

Another effect of intensive farming is the increased dependency on chemical pesticides, which kill not only the insects against which they are directed but also many others which are beneficial rather than harmful. Often the local extermination of one species of pest leads to the multiplication of another due to the incidental elimination of a natural predator. Moreover, birds are poisoned by the insecticides when they eat fruits that

have been sprayed or the poisoned insects themselves, or else those dependent upon an insect diet die out as they are deprived of their natural source
of food. As long ago as 1962, Rachel Carson's *Silent Spring* gave evidence of
the effects on birdlife of DDT and other insecticides used agriculturally.

Crop raising, however, is only one branch of agriculture, the other is
livestock farming. In earlier times this was carried on without undue harm
to the environment, but today it is a cause of major damage. As grain
harvests have increased following the green revolution, so has animal
farming, with grain being used as additional feed. And in the poorer
countries, where grain is not available as feed, overgrazing and the need in
the drier areas to drive cattle long distances to water, further exacerbate
erosion. The consequences have been unexpectedly devastating. Alan Thein
Durning and Holly B. Brough write in *State of the World—1992*:

> Rings of barren earth spread out from wells on the grasslands of
> Botswana. Heather wilts in the nature preserves of the southern
> Netherlands. Forests teeming with rare forms of life explode in flame
> in Costa Rica. Water tables fall in the United States. Each of these cases
> of environmental decline springs from a single source: the global
> livestock industry.[4]

And these are by no means all. Animal waste pollutes rivers and groundwater; it also generates methane, one of the more virulent greenhouse gases in
the atmosphere; nitrogen from manure combines with atmospheric gases
producing ammonia and is a contributing cause of acid rain. Nitrates from
manure also penetrate into groundwater to cause diseases like methemoglo-
binemia (blue baby syndrome) and cancer in humans. Overgrazing is a
main cause of erosion and desertification, while the destruction of forests to
make room for more pastures adds to the environmental destruction. Latin
America has lost twenty million hectares of tropical forests to cattle pasture
since 1970, with knock on effects of land degradation, because the exposed
soil is shallow, acidic, and low in nutrients, so that weeds abound and the
pasture soon becomes unusable, leading to further ravaging of the forests.
The United Nations Food and Agriculture Organization has reported that
Central America alone has lost more than a third of its tropical forests since
the early 1960s.[5]

In the United States the consumption of beef is prodigious. In 1991 fast
food shops alone sold six billion hamburgers, to say nothing of other diners
and restaurants. A United Nations report shows that 85 percent of cattle
ranges in the United States is being steadily destroyed by overgrazing.
Jeremy Rifkin, in the *New York Times* of 23 March 1992, reveals that nearly
half the water used every year in the United States is needed to grow feed

for livestock. According to a study by the California Department of Water Resources, it requires more than 1,200 gallons of water to produce an eight-ounce boneless steak. Cattle, in the United States alone, consume more than 70 percent of the grain harvest, and in the world as a whole about one-third. In this way millions of people, the world over, are deprived of adequate nourishment, as grain is fed to cattle, while people, especially in Africa, starve.

FISHERY

Another primary source of food is fish, the burgeoning demand for which in recent decades has induced fishermen to adopt modernized methods which have so decimated the fish stocks in many of the fishing grounds that whole species are in danger of extinction. Cod and salmon stocks off the Newfoundland coasts have virtually disappeared and illegal overfishing beyond Canadian coastal waters is depleting them even further.

Devastation has been wrought in the North Sea by fishing vessels using nets that scour the seabed and destroy the breeding grounds of some species. Overfishing has had drastic effects on stocks. More damage to the breeding places of certain species, like salmon, that migrate up rivers to mate, has occurred through pollution and damming for reservoirs or hydro-electric energy production, so that the fish populations are further threatened. Enormous drift nets, sometimes thirty miles long, strung out to catch tuna, along with all and sundry, capture and kill unnecessarily important and valued aquatic mammals, especially dolphins. And the decimation of whale populations, threatening the extinction of some varieties altogether, has become a matter of grave concern.

Measures have been taken to counteract some of these excesses, but the legislation enacted by any one country is ineffective in others, and solutions to the problems can be found only in international cooperation. But, as we shall later have reason to observe, international agreements are difficult to reach and their observance even more difficult to ensure. The economies of many maritime countries and the livelihood of millions of people, quite apart from the demand for sustenance by millions more, depend on fishing, which draws upon a highly important part of the food chain that cries out for protection and conservation.

INDUSTRY

Increase of population leads to burgeoning demands for manufactured goods of all kinds, and that again to the growth of industries which require greater consumption of energy, most of it derived from fossil fuels. Mechanized industries all over the world belch out thousands of tons of pollutants into the atmosphere daily, probably the most dangerous of which, in the long run, is carbon dioxide, the main greenhouse gas. Burning some kinds of coal and oil also emits sulphur compounds and produces acid rain, which destroys forests, damages crops (including the sugar maples of the northeastern United States), and pollutes rivers and lakes, decimating all kinds of aquatic species. Other gases, such as ozone, nitrogen oxides, and carbon monoxide, along with volatile organic compounds, are discharged into the atmosphere and combine under the influence of sunlight to form numerous other compounds. These, together with minute suspended particles of ash, soot, dust, and liquid droplets of various kinds, create smog, which has become a serious problem for many large cities, notably Los Angeles, and especially Mexico City, for it causes respiratory ailments, like asthma and lung diseases, as well as cancer, and presents many other hazards to human health.

Refineries, chemical plants, dry-cleaning concerns, and other industries required to fulfill the needs of growing urban and rural populations are the source of most of the toxins in the atmosphere. Nor is air pollution confined to cities and the wealthier countries. It is spreading to the countryside and to the poorer nations. Unhealthy levels of ozone have been detected in rural Maine and serious atmospheric pollution has occurred in Eastern Europe and the Third World, in Prague, in Bombay, and in Bangkok.[6]

Refrigerators and air-conditioning systems use chlorofluorocarbons (CFCs), which, when they are released into the air, as happens especially when old and used-up appliances are scrapped, percolate into the upper atmosphere, where they combine with (and so remove) the ozone that shields the Earth's surface from ultraviolet rays. Excessive exposure to ultraviolet light is fatal to many plants and crops and causes skin cancer and cataracts in human beings. Already a large hole in the ozone layer has been detected over the Antarctic and alarming thinning over the Northern Hemisphere has induced some governments to accelerate steps to reduce the production of CFCs. But those already in the atmosphere will last for many years, and the use of CFCs will continue for many years among underdeveloped nations, whose economies are too poor to permit the use of substitutes, unless far-reaching international action can be taken to assist them. Meanwhile, doubts remain whether the reduction of the ozone layer is not already irreversible.

People need houses, and the construction industry among others consumes large quantities of timber. Citizens nowadays also seek information and read newspapers, which, especially in the United States, grow ever more and more voluminous; and paper is made from wood pulp. The result is systematic destruction of forests in the temperate zone, in addition to the vast exploitation of the rain forests occasioned by the demand for hardwoods, without regard for the environmental impact. Only 5 percent of the original forests in the United States still remain, and in the Pacific Northwest all unprotected old-growth forests will be gone by the year 2023. These forests have been described as the lungs of the Earth, because they breathe in the CO_2 from the atmosphere and breathe out oxygen. Furthermore, they are unique, irreplaceable ecosystems, in which the region's soil and water resources are preserved, and the climate stabilized, providing habitat for many rare plants, animals, and birds (for instance, the northern spotted owl). As wanton destroyers of rain forests, the Japanese have been egregious culprits, felling enormous areas in Indonesia and elsewhere; and this devastation is additional to the slashing and burning that has been perpetrated to extend agricultural and pastoral land, all with grave consequences (which we shall presently discuss further) for life on Earth in general and for human beings in particular. Depradation of the forests has been made easier by the development of power tools that enable loggers to fell whole groves in the time that was once needed to fell a single tree. As a result, new methods of forest management have proved ever more destructive with what are now becoming disastrous consequences.

Mining

Industry today is highly mechanized and so requires vast quantities of metal of all kinds for its plants, besides what it converts into articles and appliances for general use. Moreover, to drive machines energy is needed, and this for the most part comes from fossil fuels. For both these reasons mining has become an expanding industry with its own peculiar problems and significantly shattering effects on the environment. Not long ago, there were widespread misgivings about the possible exhaustion of reserves both of ores and of oil needed to serve the growing needs of a proliferating population, but this has given place more recently to even greater concern about the human and ecological damage that is associated with mining activities: devastation of areas of natural beauty, polluted waters, expulsion of indigenous peoples from their traditional habitation, and disruption of natural fauna and flora that are vital not only to these peoples but to mankind as a whole.

Since the industrial revolution in the eighteenth century, which was the occasion for increased mining, the use of minerals has grown in conjunction with population, but has greatly outstripped it. In the century and a half before 1900 world population doubled while the use of minerals increased by a factor of ten. During the present century that has again multiplied thirteen times more. John E. Young writes:

> Annual production of pig iron—the crude metal that is usually converted into steel—now stands at 552 million tons, 22,000 times what it was in 1700. Outputs of copper and zinc are 560 and 7,300 times greater than in 1800. Although aluminum was not available commercially until 1845 and was far too expensive for large-scale production until the modern electrolytic process was invented in 1886, smelters currently turn out 18 million tons of the metal each year.[7]

Of all industries mining is the most destructive and defaces nature the most. With modern machinery it does so vastly more rapidly and on a scale immeasurably greater than ever before. It is a copious source of hazardous waste, it produces great scars on the face of the landscape, it pollutes rivers and the atmosphere, chokes streams, kills vegetation, and poisons animals that live on the plant life it contaminates. From many mines arsenic, lead, zinc, cadmium, and other poisonous substances seep into rivers and reservoirs to impair the local drinking water, and many extraction processes involve poisonous substances such as mercury and cyanide, which are collected into ponds, spilled into rivers, or, saturated in finely ground waste, heaped into piles, from which the substances are blown by wind, to pollute soil and air as well as water. In this manner, mining becomes one of the main sources (indeed, perhaps the worst) of hazardous waste, the disposal of which has nowadays emerged as one of the most urgent, yet most intractable, of problems.

Mining devastates huge areas of countryside. Two examples of the creation of yawning "dead zones" are 10,400 hectares around the Sudbury nickel smelter in Ontario and 7,000 hectares around Copper Hill in Tennessee. Japan has sacrificed 6,700 hectares of rice-producing land to mining which has made the soil unfit for cultivation; in Great Britain hundreds of thousands of acres of agricultural land have been lost to mining.

Smelting, especially of copper, spews out millions of tons of sulphur dioxide into the air, which produces minute droplets of sulphuric acid and creates acid rain, destroying forests and crops as well as aquatic life. Mining is destructive of forests in other ways as well. John Young tells how wood-fired smelters ate up the local Sussex woods in England, and how, from the same cause, smelting became "the tomb of the forests of the Sierras" in Nevada in the late nineteenth century. In Brazil, at the present time, mining enterprises at Carajas will consume 2.4 million tons of charcoal a year, requiring the felling of 50,000 hectares of forest annually, and this is projected to continue for 250 years. Other Brazilian undertakings, mining seven different kinds of mineral, will involve processing plants, hydroelectric dams, and deep-water ports, using up vast quantities of electrical energy and causing untold environmental damage to rivers and forests.

In the course of all this exploitation of the Earth's mineral wealth, the eviction of indigenous people from their traditional homelands and the attendant suffering they experience is largely forgotten. The life-style of these tribes is integrated with the natural processes of the regions in which they live, and they are not destructive of the forests they inhabit, but rather they tend to conserve the local environment. When they lose their traditional heritage, however, not only is their place taken by others who disturb the ecology, but the original inhabitants are not adequately compensated (if at all) for loss of land and possessions, and they become impoverished vagrants, or, like the Yanomami of the Amazon, are dying out, while miners take over their ancestral lands.

Yet minerals are indispensable to most of the industries on which we depend for a civilized life, and their production and export is commonly a vital factor in the economic development of the countries in which they are found. Brazil is a case in point, where so much environmental destruction is threatened by mining, as well as by pastoral expansion, for these developments are urgently needed to keep the nation solvent. The ecological disruption, however, does not affect Brazil and her neighbors alone, but, as we shall emphasize again later, menaces the balance of nature not only in the Western and Southern hemispheres, but in the world as a whole.

ENERGY

Contemporary civilization differs from earlier civilizations in that it has expanded to encompass the whole world and that it is predominantly scientific and technical. The technical revolution that began in Britain in the eighteenth century has advanced and invaded all other countries and continents, transforming the habits and ways of life of the peoples and now also the landscape. The immediate prospect is that it will soon transform the climate as well, but of that more anon. Energy is something we cannot do without, but the sources of supply, other than the natural muscular energy of ourselves and domesticated animals, have brought with them disadvantages that are now arousing grave concern.

Industry needs prodigious supplies of energy, while it also supplies energy for household purposes and public amenities. Much of this comes from fossil fuels, which, when burned, emit CO_2, and that is a main cause of global warming. Today, however, the most widely used form of energy is electricity, although coal, fuel oil, petroleum, and natural gas are all significant contributors. All of these emit great quantities of greenhouse gases into the atmosphere, and some are also the source of other harmful emissions. For this and other reasons (cost being one) many nations have, since 1960, turned to nuclear power, which, as we shall presently observe, brings its own disadvantages.

The top twelve oil-producing countries in 1990 pumped out 44.51 million barrels a day. Much of this had to be transported overseas in enormous tankers, which are occasionally wrecked and then spill out millions of gallons of oil that pollute the ocean, kill fish and birdlife, and threaten the survival of plankton, the basic food for many species and the base of the food chain for humans. Further oil spills from pipelines and refineries have, in recent years, been the cause of enormous environmental damage, and those occasioned by the Gulf War, along with the burning of hundreds of Kuwaiti oil wells, amounted at the time to a major ecological disaster.

Originally developed for military purposes, nuclear power has been adapted for ordinary, more peaceful employment. Its civilian use grew spectacularly until about 1979, when alarm was spread by the Three Mile Island nuclear meltdown, and concern mounted further in 1986, when the nuclear power plant at Chernobyl exploded. Meanwhile, nuclear power plants have been found to present risks to the health of their employees and to the surrounding population. Greater than average incidence of leukemia, especially in the children of workers at the plants, has been recorded at Sellafield in Britain, and elsewhere.

The whole issue of energy supply today presents mankind with one of its most difficult and complicated problems. The burning of fossil fuels produces greenhouse gases increasing global warming, but nuclear energy poses even greater hazards from accidents spreading deadly radioactive substances that remain toxic for thousands of years, from leakage of such substances, and from the so-far unsolved problem of nuclear waste disposal.

HAZARDOUS WASTE

The disposal of waste of all kinds has become a headache for administrators from town halls to capitols. The accumulation of rubbish in spreading conurbations has nowadays got to the stage at which no further space can be found safely or healthfully to contain the swelling mountains of refuse. Industrial waste, much of it toxic, cannot be disposed of without widespread pollution of rivers, soil, and air. Even waste that is not immediately dangerous, old cars and scrap iron, grows and expands until the dumps become eyesores and scenes of desolation. To all this must now be added the disposal of mounting quantities of radioactive waste from nuclear installations, both military and civilian.

Radiation, aside from burns and skin ulcers, has been found to cause cancer, leukemia, cataracts, mental retardation, and genetic diseases. Exposure to even quite low levels can be dangerous, in fact, some scientists say that there is no safe lower limit and that the available evidence shows any radiation, however small, to be a risk because the effects are cumulative. High-level radioactive waste remains dangerous for thousands of years. The half-life (the time it takes for half the original material to decay) of some isotopes (such as plutonium) is 24,000 years, of others as much as 710,000.

Wastes from military installations have already contaminated air, water, vegetation, and wildlife in many areas. Nobody has yet discovered any really safe way of disposing of the ever mounting quantities. Konrad Krauskopf maintains that "no scientist or engineer can give an absolute guarantee that radioactive waste will not someday leak in dangerous quantities from even the best repositories."[8] It must be housed in impenetrable containers, which will not corrode or leak for thousands of years, and none have yet been invented that are entirely dependable. It cannot be dumped in the sea, for fear that its housing will corrode and leak, which would make water and fish radioactive and would contaminate an important human food source. The Irish Sea has become so radioactive from leakages intermittently occurring at the Sellafield nuclear plant that bathing beaches can no longer be used with safety. If nuclear waste is buried deep in the earth, there is the possibility that containers may at some time be fractured by earthquakes. If water collects in contact with heated containers explosions of steam could rival volcanic eruptions. Even leakage due to less spectacular causes, always possible at some stage, is liable to affect groundwater and soils and so prove hazardous to human health. Whatever scheme is devised, and wherever the disposal is contemplated, there are risks, and if the site is, or is near, a populated area, the local people will always strenuously resist its use. Consequently, the problem of waste disposal, both hazardous and other, remains unsolved and intractable.

CITIES

People need shelter and housing, and as populations increase so does migration from the country to the towns. More and more people congregate in cities and all too soon urban sprawl eats into the countryside and industrial sites invade fields. Marcia Lowe, writing in *State of the World—1992*, records that at the beginning of this century only one-tenth of the world's population lived in cities, but if present trends continue more than half will be city dwellers by its end. "In industrial and developing countries alike," she continues, "chaotic, uncontrolled urban growth—whether measured in rising numbers or in the amount of space humans spread out upon—draws ever more land, water, and energy from surrounding regions to meet people's needs."[9]

City populations are not only increased by migration but also swelled by internal procreation, and the disconcerting results range from currently irremediable smog affliction (as in Mexico City and Los Angeles), and accumulation of perilous waste (as in Alexandria), to the draining off of underground water, such as is causing Venice, Bangkok, Shanghai, and Jakarta to sink and to suffer flooding at high tides. Feeding the city dwellers requires more agricultural production, but the spread of urban development encroaches continuously on arable land.

Cities consume water and energy in ever increasing volume, and make ever heavier demands on agriculture, fishing, and forestry, but perhaps today the most difficult and urgent problem that they face is transportation, with ever growing traffic jams, air pollution, death-dealing accidents, and noise. Especially in America first consideration is given to cars, delivery vans, trucks, and their drivers, while pedestrians tend to be overlooked.

The planning of most cities has been seriously at fault for several decades. Urban sprawl has given rise to suburban developments extending far out from the cities' centers. In the absence of efficient public transport systems commuters have to rely on private cars, which is good for the motor industry, but creates major traffic problems for inner cities and adds to atmospheric pollution. The exhaust from automobiles not only contributes to smog, and, where legislation does not compel the use of lead-free petroleum, poisons the air we breathe, it also contains a significant percentage of carbon dioxide. Every day millions of tons of this gas are pumped into the atmosphere by many millions of motor vehicles, adding to the greenhouse effect and contributing to global warming.

At the same time the increasing numbers of vehicles creates a growing demand for new and bigger roads and highways which desecrate the beauties of the landscape, further decrease the area of cultivable land, disturb the habitats of wildlife and birds, and augment the disruption of the ecology.

TOURISM

People need recreation and amusement and one very important provision of both comes from tourism. As populations grow the demand for holidays increases and as methods of transport have become more rapid and more available the number who seek holidays abroad in ever more distant localities has risen spectacularly. The result has been a widespread development of the tourist industry, with the construction of phalanxes of hotels along seafronts and in mountain resorts, the establishment of recreation facilities in wilderness areas reserved as national parks, and the setting up of lidos and marinas. Motor cruisers have multiplied by the thousand along scenic coasts, lakes have become crowded with water-skiers, climbers hike in droves over scenic hills and uplands, ski resorts abound in the higher mountains, orienteers flock to outlying countrysides, and regiments of ramblers range over fields and through woodlands.

What all this does to the environment is distressing. Paths up hillsides become worn broad and deep permitting erosion and increased weathering; plant life is destroyed; habitats of wild animals, shy of humans, some of them rare and endangered from other causes, are invaded; beauty spots are ravaged; the wash of speedboats erodes shorelines; ancient remains, like the Parthenon in Athens, are worn down by sightseers' feet, while others, such as Stonehenge, are commercialized and thronged with sightseers. Wetlands, the home of thousands of species of birds, mammals, and amphibians, and the gathering points for many migrants, are drained for "development," or plundered by hunters and fishers (when this has not already occurred for agriculture). More roads for more cars carve up the countryside, and remote haunts, attractive for their peace and tranquil beauty, are overrun by ever growing crowds of visitors. In addition the increase of air and road traffic not only creates congestion but also enhances atmospheric pollution.

All these untoward developments follow directly from the egregious growth of population during the last century and the natural and, for the most part, legitimate quest of ordinary people for food, shelter, warmth, comfort, and amusement. We read in the first chapter of Genesis that God blessed mankind and bade them "Be fruitful, and multiply, and replenish the earth, and subdue it." This they have done in full measure, but the promised blessing that should go with their proliferation looks very dubious. Before we contemplate future prospects in more detail, let us consider the broader aspects of the effects flowing from the current conditions we have been reviewing.

Notes

1. Cf. J. M. Harris, *World Agriculture and the Environment* (New York and London: Garland Publishing, Inc., 1990), pp. 110–11.
2. Cf. A. Gore, *The Earth in the Balance: Ecology and the Human Spirit* (New York, Boston, and London: Houghton Mifflin, 1992), p. 3.
3. Cf. Worldwatch, *State of the World—1992*, Annual Worldwatch Report (London: W. W. Norton and Co., 1992), p. 24.
4. Ibid., p. 66.
5. Cf. *State of the World—1992*, p. 74.
6. Cf. A. Hammond, ed., *The 1992 Environmental Almanac*, compiled by World Resources Institute (Boston, MA: Houghton Mifflin, 1992), pp. 147 ff.
7. *State of the World—1992*, chap. 7, p. 101; cf. also R. Bosson and B. Varon, *The Mining Industry and Developing Countries* (New York and London: Oxford University Press, 1977).
8. K. Krauskopf, "Disposal of High-Level Nuclear Waste," *Science* (14 September 1990).
9. Cf. *State of the World—1992*, p. 119; United Nations, *World Urbanization Prospects* (New York: UN Publications, 1991).

2

The Tale of
the Scalded Frog

INTERRELATION OF PROBLEMS

The many interactive and mutually reinforcing menaces now bearing down upon the human race all stem from exceeding population growth. Their overall consequences affect the planet as a whole, not simply one region or one race. It is the global character of the problems facing mankind that is new and unprecedented, and it is with that prominently in mind that they should be addressed. Let us then consider them briefly with the emphasis upon their comprehensive scope.

The population explosion has immediate effects that spring from the spread of urbanization, such as intensification of agricultural production, multiplication of recreational facilities, and accumulation of waste, which lead to the destruction of habitats, the endangering of species, deforestation, and loss of topsoil, with the consequent tendency to desertification. But the key factor in environmental deterioration is pollution, brought about by human activities, industry, and energy use—pollution of soil, water, and air. This has more widespread effects which intensify those already occurring, so that the process set in train by pollution is further reinforced.

THE NECESSITY FOR SPECIES DIVERSITY

It has now been scientifically established that the planet is a single ecosystem, with all living species subsisting in symbiosis, each dependent on many others, and in the last resort on all the rest. This applies just as much to mankind as to other species, although we have habitually thought of ourselves as set apart, superior (as in some important ways we are), and

17

independent of surrounding nature, which we think we are at liberty to exploit for our own benefit. No such conception can be entertained any longer. If we are to have any hope for survival we must realize immediately and vividly our unity with and dependence upon nature as a whole, and upon all other species, however remote they may seem, however obscure or apparently insignificant.

Nobody knows how many living species exist on Earth. There may be as many as 80 million, and probably not less than 10 million, of which scientists have discovered fewer than 1.5 million. Of these it is estimated that, at the present time, 140 species of invertebrate animals and at least one species of plant, reptile, bird, mammal, or fish are exterminated *every day*.[1] The causes of this dereliction are first and foremost the destruction of the forests in which about half the living species on the planet find their home, and of which already half the original area has been destroyed. The second most important habitat is wetlands, now threatened, or already eliminated, by drainage for agriculture, urban development, industrial demands, and similar pressures. Of these more than 90 percent in developed, and a rapidly growing proportion in developing, countries have already gone, and human pursuits are encroaching upon what remain. Water pollution is yet another cause of species loss in the wetlands of the world, not to mention acquaculture, and the silting up of estuaries due to soil erosion. In comparison to these losses, the ravages of hunting and uncontrolled fishing pale almost into insignificance although they are by no means negligible.

It is obvious that human beings depend for food on many of the species now under threat, and these again depend for their survival on others in what is called the continuous food chain. The preservation of biological diversity is, therefore, of the utmost importance for life on Earth. Nor is it only the food chain that is vital for survival. Inbreeding weakens progeny, while interbreeding between different varieties strengthens the stock. Lack of diversity, therefore, is apt to debilitate the species, as has happened to many kinds of fish on the West Coast of America, and of trees where natural forests have been replaced by plantations of a single commercial variety. The reduction of diversity, for instance, in grain, where varieties have been ousted to make room for new high-yield types, has exposed crops to diseases and pests against which the lost varieties were, or could become, resistant, and which now are liable to ravage enormous areas, where at one time they could have been confined within manageable limits. The original wild varieties of most of the world's important crops are concentrated in only a few places (about twelve), in different parts of the world, all of which are now being threatened environmentally, or have already been largely destroyed by drought, desertification, or some similar deleterious agency, and attempts to counteract this loss of genetic diversity by the development of gene banks has had little official support from governments, is very ill organized, and is grossly underfunded.[2]

The use of pesticides, as we have noted, is a virulent cause of species decimation, destroying not only the verminous kinds, but also those that feed on them, as well as others quite innocent that are inadvertently poisoned. Likewise, intensive farming methods deprive wildlife of habitats, and intensive fishing exterminates valuable, beautiful, and much needed species.

But it is pollution that causes most of the damage: pollution of earth and soil, causing disease or immediate poisoning; of water, making wetlands uninhabitable and destroying fish and vegetable life in streams and lakes, depriving ducks and waders of their provender, as well as gulls and ospreys; of the atmosphere, with even more ominous and potentially devastating consequences (to which we shall return), the most far-reaching being climate change, with which many species, already adapted to the zone they now inhabit, are unable to keep pace, and cannot migrate quickly enough to escape.

DEFORESTATION

Perhaps the most calamitous of all forms of environmental damage is the execrable loss of the rain forests. We have already observed how prodigious the destruction has been. And the most frightening thought is that the rain forests are the chief source of oxygen in the Earth's atmosphere. It is oxygen that we breathe, that supports the combustion of the fuels which give us warmth and energy, and without which most life cannot endure. Moreover, the forests absorb carbon dioxide and maintain the balance of atmospheric gases. It is the excessive increase in CO_2 more than any other gas that creates the greenhouse effect and gives rise to global warming. Further, the forests transpire vast quantities of water vapor that cools the air and keeps the temperature tolerable, even (or especially) in the tropics. It replenishes the clouds and maintains rainfall, affecting the climate the world over. Deforestation thus causes widespread drought and contributes to the encroachment of deserts upon arable land and pasturage, which today, especially in Africa, is causing mass undernourishment and starvation. Reduction of rainfall in part of the Amazon Basin has produced unprecedentedly dry conditions in the forest itself, so that biologists fear a gigantic and uncontrollable conflagration if it should accidentally be set alight. The forests themselves depend upon rain, and they give back to the atmosphere the water they drink from the soil; but logging, slashing, and burning, by reducing the forest area, leads not only to soil exhaustion and erosion, but reduces the rainfall, and so endangers the forest that remains.

DESERTIFICATION

What was once known as the breadbasket of the Roman Empire is now the Sahara Desert. Today overgrazing, overcultivation, soil exhaustion, and denudation of topsoil is creating new deserts and extending old ones in almost every continent. While population grows apace, agricultural and pastoral lands are shrinking, so that more and more people go hungry. As with deforestation, so the creation of deserts is a self-reinforcing process: more desert means less rainfall; reduced rainfall creates more desert. Droughts in Africa are becoming more frequent and more prolonged as the years pass, and much the same is occurring in parts of California, South America, Asia, and Australia; and not even Europe is immune. A major contributing cause, however, with reciprocal enhancing effects is global warming, another result of pollution, to which we shall now turn our attention.

ATMOSPHERIC POLLUTION

James Lovelock has put forward the hypothesis that the Earth as a whole is a single organism, and Lewis Thomas has compared it to a living cell.[3] The atmosphere functions like the protective membrane of the cell, regulating the Earth's energy intake from the Sun and protecting it from harmful radiation, regulating its temperature and circulating life-supporting substances. The ozone layer in the upper atmosphere filters out ultraviolet radiation and protects living things on the Earth's surface from its deleterious effects. This sensitive membrane is now being seriously damaged by the current practices of human civilized living.

To many plants ultraviolet radiation is lethal and in humans and other animals it causes blindness, cataracts, and skin cancer. Chlorofluorocarbons manufactured by man and released into the air, ascend to the ozone layer and destroy it, exposing the creatures below to the dire effects of ultraviolet radiation. The thinning of the ozone layer has by now proceeded far enough to have alarmed the governments of Britain and the United States into decreeing strict limitation of the production of CFCs; but the effects of these gases will continue, even after all production has ceased. Measurements of CFCs in the atmosphere made in 1991 have shown a slight decrease (about 2 percent), but this is only of some and not all the varieties.

Those that remain are expected to last for from 50 to 100 years. Meanwhile some substances used as substitutes are themselves destructive of the ozone layer, and scientists speculate whether the damage may not already have become irreversible. This form of atmospheric pollution, therefore, poses a serious threat to human health, and, as it destroys crops, to human survival.

Emissions that create smog, inhalation of which impairs human health in other ways, are more localized in their impact. But among them are the greenhouse gases that trap the sun's heat and raise the average temperature of the entire planet, with manifold and far-reaching results that augur catastrophe on a worldwide scale. There is now fairly conclusive evidence that global warming has actually occurred and is increasing.

> Some scientists predict an average surface temperature increase of up to 9° Fahrenheit in the next 100 years, which is comparable to the temperature difference between the extreme climate of the last ice age 18,000 years ago and today's climate.

So reports the World Resources Institute.[4] Christopher Flavin records that CO_2 concentrations in the atmosphere were 354 parts per million in 1990, while global temperatures have reached the highest levels of the past century.[5] This level of CO_2 content is 30 percent higher than in the preindustrial era. One billion tons of CO_2 a year enters the atmosphere from the burning of tropical forests alone, while transportation (motor vehicles and aircraft) and electric power generation together account for more than half the CO_2 emissions from fossil fuels.

Other warming gases are methane (constituting 12 percent to carbon dioxide's 54 percent, but contributing a disproportionately greater greenhouse effect), nitrous oxide, CFCs, ozone, and other trace gases. It is clear that the prospective global warming trend is the result of human activities, and it is human activity that must be enlisted if it is to be counteracted and, if possible, reversed. This is still feasible, if appropriate action is taken with sufficient promptness, but it will require drastic changes in lifestyles, methods of production, and economic and political policies.

There is no clear consensus about the probable effects of global warming, other than that, whatever they may be, they will cause quite stupendous climatic changes. Only a relatively small increase in global temperature is sufficient to melt a significant proportion of the polar ice, which already has been found noticeably thinner in the north than a few years ago. Such melting will raise the level of the oceans, and a rise of only a few feet will be enough to inundate low-lying coastal areas, where half the world's population live. The eastern United States, Bangladesh, and Indonesia are only a few of the states that would suffer. Many of the most populous and historic cities would be flooded, and small islands in the Indian and Pacific oceans would be altogether submerged. The warming effect would, moreover, be intensified by an exceptional thaw in the northern polar region, because some greenhouse gases (methane, in particular) now trapped in the arctic ice would be released.

Sharp differences in pressure and temperature will produce greater atmospheric turbulence, causing violent storms in places not hitherto subject to extreme weather conditions. This has already occurred in such unwonted places as the south coast of England, where hurricane-force winds swept across the southern counties a few years ago. Hurricanes and cyclones would increase in frequency and violence, doing even greater damage than they already do.

Temperate climates would become more tropical, and arctic conditions would become more temperate. Some kinds of flora would succumb to new and uncongenial conditions and others would thrive where they could not before. Many animal and plant species would have to change their habitat, but, because the climate change is now occurring faster than any that has occurred in the past several thousand years, they might fail to do so in time to save themselves from extinction. All this is possible within the next few decades if present trends continue at the rate already detected.

It has been suggested that global warming could be an advantage, if arctic tundra, for example, becomes suitable for agriculture. Unfortunately, no such optimism is justified, because the deep permafrost of the tundra would not melt and would prevent the growth of crops. Moreover, it is clear that any possible marginal advantage would be greatly outweighed by the destructive effects of the enormous and relatively rapid climatic changes that would occur worldwide, signs of which are already being detected.

The predictions are based on computer models, and not all such models agree. Some, in fact, predict conditions almost opposite to those above described. Higher temperatures, it is presumed, will increase evaporation, and that will generate excessive cloud cover, shutting out sunlight and warmth, so that the ground temperature will actually fall dramatically and initiate a new ice age. This may sound somewhat incredible, but whichever prognostication one accepts the prospect is grim, and the one point on which all agree is that global warming is actually happening. Six of the hottest years in over a century have been recorded between 1983 and 1991, with average temperatures rising all the time.

Other prognostications are even more alarming; they predict differential climate change, with warming occurring in the lower latitudes while cooling occurs in the upper latitudes. This would bring on ice age conditions more rapidly still, and widespread crop failures that would cause famine throughout the world and threaten starvation on an enormous scale within the next few decades. The extreme urgency of the situation can hardly be exaggerated, and the need for prompt action to counteract the trends cannot be too strongly emphasized.

TAKING STOCK

Sandra Postel, in the first chapter of *State of the World—1992*, has summarized the world situation as follows (I am not following the order she adopts):

World population is growing by 92 million people annually. Of this total 88 million are being added in the developing world.

The protective ozone shield in heavily populated latitudes of the northern hemisphere is thinning twice as fast as scientists thought just a few years ago.

A minimum of 140 plant and animal species are condemned to extinction each day.

Atmospheric levels of heat-trapping carbon dioxide are now 26 percent higher than in the preindustrial concentration, and continue to climb.

The earth's surface was warmer in 1990 than in any year since record keeping began in the mid-nineteenth century; six of the seven warmest years on record have occurred since 1980.

Forests are vanishing at a rate of some 17 million hectares per year, an area half the size of Finland.

Beset though we are by so many and such complex and interconnected crises, however, the situation is not yet hopeless, even if its desperate urgency is obvious. There are feasible remedies to most of these pressing and multiplying ills, which could save the planet if they were expeditiously and comprehensively applied. First, and most imperative, is the necessary change from fossil fuels to renewable energy sources. This is by no means impracticable. Natural gas can be substituted for petroleum, and it releases far less damaging exhaust. Although its use would not finally solve our energy problems, the first step in the right direction would seem to be to turn to it as a substitute for other fuels. Transition from natural gas to hydrogen would then be possible by methods already projected by engineers, and hydrogen burns without any detrimental atmospheric emission. Solar and wind energy are harmless and renewable, and already they are contributing in some places to the provision of electricity; and the same is true of energy derived from the tides and from biothermal sources. What is urgently needed is increased funding for more intensive research into the methods of using these resources, so that they can replace coal and oil as energy providers. Christopher Flavin, writing in *State of the World—1992*, contends:

> The solar-hydrogen economy is compellingly simple in design, economically practical, and ecologically necessary. Moreover, it does not require any radical scientific breakthroughs or discovery of entirely new resources. This vision of the possible may finally spark an energy revolution. If so, the pace of change could surprise us all.[6]

Other expedients are called for to stop the destruction of the rain forests and, if possible, to renew their growth. It is also necessary to change agricultural methods, and to reform our dietary habits, to decrease the consumption of meat; and none of these policies are impracticable. The disposal of hazardous waste would be more difficult, but reliance on nuclear energy should be reduced as other renewable sources become available, and that would at least stem the flow of nuclear waste. In general, it may be said that it should not be beyond the intellectual powers of mankind, nor should it defeat our ingenuity, to overcome these problems. But we must act quickly and in concert if we are to succeed.

CONDITIONS OF SUCCESS

What should be recognized, but is not widely admitted, is that no remedies are likely to be effective if they are not universally applied. The problems are global and local expedients will not remove them. The use of wind power in California and solar power in Arizona may mitigate the accumulation of greenhouse gases, but it cannot altogether prevent global warming. Emission of CO_2 from fossil fuel burning, wherever it occurs, affects the Earth's atmosphere as a whole. Reducing it in one region will not help if it is increased or maintained in another. The destruction of the ozone shield exposes not just one, but many, nations to ultraviolet radiation; so the decision by the Europeans or the Americans to phase out the production of CFCs will not protect them if undeveloped countries continue to use them. The damage done by the Chernobyl explosion was not confined to the Ukraine, nor would the effects of any other nuclear accident that might occur. Nuclear waste from Sellafield worries the Irish even more than the English; and sulphur emissions from British coal-burning plants plague the forests of Norway with acid rain. The destruction of the rain forests is a threat to the entire world, not just to Brazil or Indonesia. Global problems demand global solutions.

Further, voluntary action is unlikely to be sufficient to cope with these matters. Corporations are too preoccupied with profits and dividends to give much heed to the environmental effects of their production methods. Legal regulation and enforcement is essential if results are to be ensured. And when several different states are involved, legislation is unlikely to be universal, or expedients to be widely adopted. Cooperation can be brought about by nothing less than international agreement; but that, we shall find, is not easy to come by, nor is conformity guaranteed, even when agreements are reached. What is indispensable is a new global world order with authority and power to legislate remedial measures.

RESISTANCE TO CHANGE

For centuries we have been encouraged by our religion and by our educators to think of human beings as somehow different from other natural creatures. Religion has taught us to think of ourselves as differing from other animals by having immortal souls. Scientists have made us believe that nature is a sort of machine put at our disposal to use and exploit in whatever ways we can devise, and the Bible (for instance, the first chapter of Genesis) seems to justify the belief. Only very recently has science discovered that the universe is a single whole, that nature is one system of interdependent parts, and that humankind is totally dependent upon the maintenance of the balance of nature for its survival. So we still tend to think we can get along quite nicely while ignoring the effect that our behavior has upon the environment, and we are reluctant to give up our habits of exploiting natural resources for our own immediate comfort and convenience, without consideration of the consequences. As a result, we find it hard to realize the nature (let alone the acuteness) of the problem that confronts us today, and we resist admitting it in all kinds of devious ways.

The changes demanded of us if the planet is to be saved are so great and so unprecedented that few are ready to accept the need for them. It is now twenty years since disturbances to the balance of nature have been noticed by scientists; yet, in spite of valiant work done by Greenpeace, taking vigorous and courageous action from Iceland to the Antarctic, despite public pronouncements and reports issued by concerned bodies, admirable books written by worried authors, and excellent nature films broadcast on television, many people seem still unaware of the multiple dangers we face.

True, there is now a growing awareness among the public that "green" issues are important, a gradually increasing realization of the fragility of the ecosystem and a more eager search than hitherto for ways of extricating mankind from the predicament in which it is placed. Even so, the majority feel that they can probably carry on more or less as usual, as long as they modify their behavior slightly in one or two respects. Perhaps the very enormity of the problem makes people unwilling to face it and prompts them to seek to deny that it exists, or, at least, to think it is not as bad as it is made out to be. This kind of denial is quite common and is perhaps the greatest danger of all, for unless swift and resolute action is taken, environmental deterioration may pass the point of no return and become irreversible. But even when people do realize the threats of impending disaster, they do not always understand their causes, still less do they appreciate the extent and nature of the changes needed to our ways of thinking and conducting our affairs for which the situation calls, especially in the international sphere.

One way of evading the pressing issues is to point to disagreement among scientists about the reported facts, or disputes as to their causes, even when the facts are admitted. Some disagreement there may be between the experts, but the salient facts are generally recognized and the main causes are well known. To appeal to scientific differences of opinion as an excuse for delaying action, therefore, is no more than an evasion of the issue. Sufficient evidence has been established to make it sheer folly to ignore the dangers and obviously prudent to take the urgently necessary steps to avert them, especially when those steps are practicable, relatively easy, and promise to be salutary.

Then again, there are vested interests that prevent some people from facing up to what may seem rather remote problems. The changes necessary are often costly, and businesspeople are distracted by cost-benefit calculations. Manufacturers fight shy of large changes to plants or the use of materials unless they see a prospect of short-term gain. It takes effort and often causes temporary inconvenience to change heating systems and manufacturing processes. Retailers tend to respond to public demand, rather than offer their customers environmentally friendly commodities. So many factors encourage such resistance that every means of publicity and advertisement is necessary to educate the population of the world and to impress upon their imaginations the severity and relentlessness of present dangers, so as to arouse and confirm their determination to take appropriate action. For it should by now be apparent that the costs of delay will far outweigh the expense and inconvenience of necessary change, and that the situation calls for immediate action.

At the moment there is little sign that the situation is being given the attention its seriousness warrants. Where today do we see any very reassuring progress in any of the indicated directions? What sign is there as yet of automobile manufacturers contemplating a changeover to natural gas engines? Who has yet seen, or what company has yet proposed, the production of electric cars, although the idea has been mooted and enthusiastically advocated by environmentalists? What encouragement do governments give to research on the harnessing of renewable energy, and how many are willing to spend money on it? Where is there any movement towards persuading people to adopt a vegetarian diet, even if there is one to promote cholesterol-free foods? What plans are evident of new environmentally friendly agricultural policies? There is virtually no evidence of progress in any of these directions, even where they are much discussed.

Certainly, there have been some promising scientific conferences, which have made significant pronouncements about impending dangers and the measures that ought to be taken to meet them; but the response from governments has been half-hearted and grudging. The British government at first agreed to legislate only to limit CO_2 emissions to current levels by 2005; and although Britain has now decided to advance that date, the American administration is still dragging its feet even more sluggishly. Meanwhile, what is needed is not simply limitation to current levels, but, as far as possible, total elimination of excessive CO_2 production.

The United Nations convened a World Summit meeting in Rio de Janeiro in June 1992, but already the United States had refused to commit itself to giving aid to developing countries unable to meet the cost of environmental policies. In fact, many environmentalists considered that the summit was destined to fail, if only because it did not represent the majority of the world's population who live in the poorer countries; they could not afford to attend, said the critics, and unless they could speak English nobody would listen to them. By April 1992 the delegates seeking to draft an agenda had achieved little success; nor did environmentalists expect that they would, because the nations, north and south, with the United States to the fore, all balked at measures which might prove difficult or costly. Few if any were thinking in terms of radical change, the wealthier states anxious about costs and the poorer ones stressing poverty above conservation of the ecology. Each put its national interests before global requirements for a safe environment. In the outcome, little was achieved. The United States refused to sign the projected Biodiversity Treaty; Japan declined even to send its prime minister to the conference, and failed to provide the expected increase in foreign aid needed to implement environmental protection by the poorer countries; the European Community environment commissioner absented himself in protest, and the European ministers for overseas development disagreed about honoring their commitment to donate .07 percent of gross domestic product for environmental preservation. Of the seventy-five billion dollars in aid sought by the undeveloped countries for environmental protection, less than one billion was promised. A general plan of action was agreed, but how it was to be financed was not determined. In sum, although certain general objectives were defined, no deadlines for reaching them were fixed, and nothing that was agreed was made legally binding. So no very encouraging prospect of decisive action has emerged.

What is clear is that the United Nations is incapable of taking effective action as long as its members consider national interests primary, and global requirements subordinate to them, as sovereign independent nations are bound to do (for reasons that will become clearer in what is to follow), whatever they may agree to undertake in conferences such as the Rio summit; and that, as events have proved, has been indecisive and niggling.

In short, there is no sign yet that people in general or their leaders are really aware of the imminence or the magnitude of the threats to human survival, nor is there any evidence of a corresponding feeling of urgency. But if determined action is not taken very soon, the race will court its own extinction, along with so many other endangered species.

CAUTIONARY TALE

The story is told of some schoolchildren who decided as part of their nature study to try an experiment. They caught a frog and threw it into a beaker of boiling water. The frog frantically leapt out of the beaker, scalded but still surviving and able to recover. Then the children placed the frog in a beaker of cold water and heated it gradually over a Bunsen burner. Now the frog found its surroundings quite congenial and was lulled to inactivity by the pleasant warmth; but as the temperature rose it became comatose and by the time the water boiled it was dead.

At the present time the human race is in an analogous situation. As a result of our own activities the world we inhabit is heating up. Until now we have been unaware of the fact and even today our attention is not much attracted to it. But if we go on ignoring it, we are in danger of suffering the fate of the frog in the fable. Nobody knows precisely what the temperature of the water in the imagined beaker would be, corresponding to the present deterioration of the global ecosystem. It is surely time for us to find out.

Notes

1. Cf. J. C. Ray, "Conserving Biological Diversity," chap. 2 in *State of the World—1992* (London: W. W. Norton and Co., 1992).
2. Cf. S. C. Witt, *Biotechnology and Genetic Diversity* (San Francisco, CA: CSI, 1985).
3. Cf. J. E. Lovelock, *Gaia: A New Look at Life on Earth* (New York and Oxford: Oxford University Press, 1979, 1987); L. Thomas, *The Lives of a Cell* (New York: Viking Press, 1974; Harmondsworth, England: Penguin Books, 1987).
4. *The 1992 Environmental Almanac*, p. 273.
5. *State of the World—1992*, p. 33.
6. *State of the World—1992*, p. 45.

3

The State
of the Nations

THE RECEDING NUCLEAR THREAT

Until very recently the most terrifying and imminent threat to the survival of mankind on this planet was the prospect of nuclear holocaust—a threat widely acknowledged, yet one that few people took as seriously as would have been appropriate. At one time it was necessary to argue at some length to persuade most people that a major nuclear war would exterminate humanity, either immediately or in the longer term (as the result of its aftereffects). Later, the prediction of a nuclear winter as the consequence of such a war was generally accepted and there was no further need, in order to convince the public that nuclear war is to be avoided at all cost, to expatiate on the widespread and catastrophic destruction from blast and fallout that would result, or the total disruption of organized (or even disorderly) life, or the reduction and poisoning of food supplies, or the devastation of everything that makes survival feasible.[1]

Now, however, this threat has receded, although it has by no means been altogether removed. It has receded because of the foresight and wisdom of the one great statesman of the age who has had the courage to take the necessary practical steps to bring about international détente: Mikhail Gorbachev, whose introduction into the Soviet Union of *glasnost* and *perestroika* transformed the face of Europe and put an end to the Cold War. It was on his initiative that a hectoring American president (who had likened the Soviets to "the Evil Empire")was persuaded to agree to sign the first significant disarmament treaty in history and to set afoot the movement to reduce nuclear arsenals. Presidents Bush and Yeltsin have since pledged themselves to reduce the numbers of nuclear warheads yet more drastically,

31

and have even suggested the substitution of a cooperative means of security for the American Strategic Defense Initiative. Hence, the threat of nuclear holocaust that had come so close is now less imminent, and the doomsday clock, already pointing to within five minutes to midnight, has been set back a quarter of an hour or so.

Nevertheless, the nuclear menace is far from having been eliminated. The United States and the new Commonwealth of Independent Republics still retain thousands of warheads, quite sufficient, if used, to produce the deprecated effects. Neither Britain nor France has shown any intention of abandoning or reducing their so-called nuclear deterrent (why "so-called" will presently appear). China, India, and Pakistan have not renounced their claims to possess, nor the right if necessary to use, nuclear weapons. Iraq came perilously near, before the Gulf War, to acquiring them. It is widely believed that Israel and South Africa have both developed nuclear capability, to which neither confess; and there are other countries still aspiring to belong to the nuclear élite. The problem of proliferation remains and nobody has yet devised any method of prevention. The newly independent republics that constituted the former Soviet Union have not all given firm assurances that they will forego the possession and use of nuclear weapons, and in dire economic predicaments they are quite likely to try to dispose of such expertise and materials as they may have to other nations eager and able to buy them for hard currency. Problems arising from the circumstances surrounding the breakup of the Soviet Union are both numerous and complicated, and the disposal, or use, of nuclear weapons is among them.

Moreover, the danger that nuclear explosives may fall into the hands of terrorists remains; and so does the very real possibility of accidents of the Chernobyl variety. Many nuclear devices belonging to the former Soviet republics are said to be in poor and hazardous condition, with nobody able to prevent their further deterioration, nor any authority with adequate means to render them secure. The effects of any such accidents on the environment and on world ecology are virtually incalculable. They can certainly not be confined within the borders of any one country, nor can measures be taken by any one government to remedy them.

THE ECONOMIC SCENE

Meanwhile world economics are in the doldrums, with few exceptions; even the economies of Japan and Germany are feeling the pinch. The collapse of the Communist states of Central Europe and of the Soviet Union has left these countries in the direst straits, seeking for help from the

West to reconstruct their industries and to establish a market economy where none (apart from the black market) has existed for decades. Their currencies are for the most part worthless and inflation is on the rampage. The Western nations, on the other hand, are experiencing a stubborn regression which, despite constant predictions of recovery, refuses to "bottom out" or else is bumping along the bottom with little, if any, sign of an upturn. Consequently, there is no great hope that the West can do much to alleviate the shortages and the confusion of the East, let alone give assistance to developing lands. The General Agreement on Tariffs and Trade has been struggling for years to live up to its name, but until now disagreement between the United States and Europe on farm subsidies has frustrated all efforts at an accord, although attempts to span what seems to be an unbridgeable gap continue.

Nations of the European Community are moving towards closer association, proposing a unified currency, and are making gestures of cautious welcome towards other states, of the former Warsaw Pact and of the Free Trade Association, to future membership; but Britain, under a Conservative government, has been pulling in the opposite direction and has strongly resisted every suggestion of anything like a federal unity, for fear of losing the sovereign right of Parliament to make its own independent decisions and of the British government to pursue its own chosen policies. The Germans are struggling with the costs and administrative difficulties of unification, exacerbated by the influx of foreign refugees from the former Yugoslavia; and the French along with other countries are faced with problems of inflation, unemployment, and consequent growing resentment against immigrant workers and refugees seeking asylum.

There is considerable confusion of thought about federal union among politicians and populace in the European Community. Resistance to closer unity and opposition to the Maastricht Treaty derive from a natural fear of outside interference in domestic affairs, which genuine federal government is designed to avoid. The structure set up by the Treaty of Rome is not federal, nor is that proposed in Maastricht. Resistance to closer union, in consequence, arises from the lack of democratic control over institutions such as the European Commission and the Council of Ministers.

Pressure for reform would be more appropriate if it concentrated on giving the European Parliament more power and making the executive bodies more responsible to it. What is also indispensable for proper federal government is a clear distinction between those matters of purely domestic interest that should be reserved to the states' jurisdiction and those of common concern to be taken over by the federal authority. A somewhat distorted recognition of this requirement is reflected in current talk about "subsidiarity." Deprecation by members of the British Conservative party (and others) against a United States of Europe, like the United States of America, is largely unreasoned and apparently uninformed. Moreover, there are other federal models to be followed, if need be, such as Switzerland, Canada and Australia; and there is nothing to prevent the adoption of new devices to meet special needs and local demands. Meanwhile, present strains within the community are prompted by devotion to what is really an outdated nationalism and an ill-founded belief in national independence, which in reality no longer exists, for in this day and age no nation is independent, economically, ecologically, or culturally.

The undeveloped countries are economically in grave difficulties even greater than those experienced by economically more advanced nations— difficulties exacerbated by overwhelming debt, the interest on which alone is crippling their exchequers, even when they are not wracked by civil wars. The drug traffic defies all attempts to arrest its activities, and is, in some cases, closely bound up with the economic survival of the producing countries. As we have seen, many attempts to introduce change have a serious detrimental effect on the environment, creating new threats to human survival.

There can be no question but that none of these dangers can be averted, and none of the problems solved, without widespread cooperation between the presently established sovereign states, none of which, by itself, has either the jurisdiction or the capacity to cope with them on its own. The likelihood and effectiveness of such cooperation is a matter we shall shortly discuss.

INTERNATIONAL FLASH POINTS

While the relations between the greater powers have, since the late 1980s, become greatly improved, there are still dangerous tensions in other parts of the world. The situation in Yugoslavia remains perilously uncertain, and persistent internecine strife in Bosnia-Herzegovina has flared up into a horrifying and intolerably vicious conflict, which could become even more widespread if no wiser counsels prevail. The dismal failure of both the European Community and the United Nations to mediate between the warring parties and to prevent the carnage and persecution is directly relevant to the argument I shall pursue in succeeding chapters. It has not been for lack of effort or good intentions, but has resulted constantly from the claim of the main combatants to sovereign independence (possibly prematurely recognized by other nations) and the inability of the international bodies to enforce the observance of agreements repeatedly entered into.

There is a very real danger that this appalling war may spill over the borders of the former Yugoslavia, involving Hungary, Greece, and Turkey, because many of the victims of the deplorable practice of "ethnic cleansing" are Muslims, and their plight has excited indignation throughout the Muslim world (which includes Turkey), while at the same time the claim of Macedonia to independence has incensed the Greeks, who claim a proprietary right to the name. If they became involved, the probability that their traditional enemies, the Turks, would be drawn in as well cannot be discounted. Sarajevo, the scene of many of the worst horrors, has in the past been the starting point of one great war; there is now considerable fear that it may be that of yet another.

Relations between the now independent republics of the former Soviet Union are far from clear or satisfactory: occasions for violence and strife persist in Nagorno-Karabakh, in Moldova, and in Georgia. Who will control the Black Sea Fleet remains uncertain, despite reported agreements about partition. The entire question of the command of the former Red Army and the organization of the previous Soviet defense system has yet to be settled. Meanwhile, all the republics of the new Commonwealth and their neighbors who have not yet joined it are suffering the most acute economic crisis, and have numerous potential causes for conflict and dispute.

In the Middle East acts of conflict and defiance recur and there are slender hopes of peace between Israel and its neighbors, notwithstanding the "peace process" sponsored by the United States and Russia and the subsequent change of government in Israel. Elsewhere in that region the problems of Iraq's aims and activities are far from having been solved. Internal contradictions and conflicts in Iran still present the West with questions affecting relations with that country; and what the future holds for Afghanistan is as yet highly questionable. A fresh dispute that flared up between Libya and the Western nations over surrendering to justice members of Colonel Qaddafi's regime suspected of implicity in terrorist acts still simmers. The colonel has done his best to blow it up into a confrontation between the West and the whole Arab world, gaining support that threatens the erstwhile cooperation between Arabs and non-Arabs in the Gulf War. His talk of a new crusade against Islam ominously threatens a new call for jihad.

The situation in Cambodia is extremely uncertain and perilous, and in Burma, where the tyranny of the military dictatorship seems to be quite unconscionable, there is repression and strife, while conditions for those in opposition to the government appear to be altogether appalling. In the Horn of Africa there is continuous disastrous fighting and widespread famine. In Somalia where there is no longer any real government, law and order has virtually disappeared in some areas, so that relief agencies are hampered and the efforts being made to feed the population are continually frustrated. The civil war in Mozambique continues to wreak havoc among the people of that country, causing increasing destitution and famine. Zaire teeters on the brink of violent revolution, presently held at bay rather precariously by the authoritarian regime of President Mobutu. And the situation in South Africa, despite some promising moves towards reform, is still highly doubtful: President de Klerk, whose good faith is looking more doubtful after revelations of police and army complicity in political terrorism, seems in no hurry to set up an interim government satisfactory to all parties, and the process of negotiation is hampered by continuing violence in the townships. There is also a far from illusory prospect of right-wing backlash and regressive terrorism with a new and ominous rapprochement between white extremists and a recalcitrant Zulu Nkatha Freedom party, aligned against the government and the African National Congress, each of which is recriminating against the other.

PERSISTENT PERILS

What all this amounts to is that there are still many potential flash points around the world where warfare already in progress could escalate, or could flare up where it is not yet occurring. That nuclear weapons, and certainly the threat of their use, might be involved is evident from the current anxieties of the major powers (repeatedly expressed by the British foreign secretary), and the worries of the United States administration about proliferation. So while the arms race between superpowers has ceased for the present, and has even taken on the appearance of a competition between them to reduce arsenals, there remain prospects of new threats that might induce them to reverse this process of relaxation.

Moreover, governments change and with them policies; unexpected and unpredictable coups may at any time overturn existing well-intentioned regimes; so the nations continue to hold on to their military power and their ability to augment it. They profess and loudly advertise the need to keep up their guard. The British prime minister, John Major, speaking on the "Today Programme" of the BBC (22 August 1991) said: "The military defence of our own interests is of first importance to any government, and especially to a Conservative government."

While economic difficulties are at the moment forcing the major powers to reduce their expenditure on defense, and the prevailing relaxation of tensions between them following upon the end of the Cold War enables them to do so with comparative safety, if conditions change for the worse, against which there is no guarantee, this trend towards disarmament and détente may well be reversed. It is therefore not surprising that the foremost nations retain large numbers of nuclear weapons, quite sufficient, if they are ever used, to bring about disaster on as great a scale as has ever been envisaged.

Accordingly, the threat of wholesale nuclear destruction (so appalling when considered in detail), although now less apparent, has not been removed, and the prospect for the human race remains as bleak as it ever has been since the Second World War. To discount or ignore this fact, simply because it is not at the moment obvious and seems to be more remote than it has been hitherto, would be as rash and as foolish as to dismiss, or be dilatory about, the environmental threat of ecological breakdown and climatic disaster. In this connection also, we should not forget the plight of the frog becoming comatose in water the temperature of which is gradually rising.

OBSTACLES TO AMELIORATION

Neither of the above menaces can be adequately countered within the limits of jurisdiction of national sovereign states, a fact not always readily admitted by politicians; and when it is recognized resort is taken to diplomacy and international agreement. This has the disadvantage that agreements are always between sovereign governments, which interpret their terms as they wish, often in conflicting and controversial ways, and always in accordance with what is seen by the party concerned as its national interest, so that the intended effect of the agreement is often nullified. Even worse is the possibility that the parties to the agreement are free at any time to renounce it, and there is no lack of cases in which commitments have been simply ignored and treaties violated as happened to suit any one of the signatories. In particular, the problem is ever-present of how to supervise and detect infringements, which occur with abundant frequency even among apparently trustworthy parties.

Here the authority of the United Nations should come into play, and indeed in the past year or so its influence seems to have been more effective than ever before. During the period of the Cold War, it could hardly ever perform its intended (or for that matter any significant) function, because resolutions of the Security Council, the main executive body, were constantly liable to the veto of one or other of the five permanent members, who belonged to opposing blocs on the political front. So frustrating was this practice that many nations had desisted altogether from appealing to the organization in cases of dispute or in circumstances of crisis. Since the cessation of the Cold War, the five permanent members of the Security Council have been in substantial agreement and have cooperated in an unprecedented manner, with the result that concerted action could be taken, for instance in dealing with Middle Eastern problems like those of Iraq and the Palestinian predicament.

With the decline of the Soviet Union and Gorbachev's revolution in foreign affairs, the Security Council has become virtually an instrument of American foreign policy. Its members followed the recommendations of the United States administration almost slavishly in the affair of the Persian Gulf, even when opinions differed between the members. China, Russia, and several European countries (France, in particular) were far less bellicose than was President Bush, and would have preferred to wait longer to test the effect of economic sanctions against Iraq before resorting to force. The American pressure for military action, however, proved irresistible. In the opinion of many, for what it is worth, the war was waged more to serve American interest in the unhampered supply of oil than in the liberation of Kuwait. Much the same has happened in the dispute with Libya over bringing to trial suspected terrorists. The demands of the United States, Britain, and France have prevailed over the objections of the Arab League and Third World states that have supported it. The suggestion that the suspects should be brought before an international court (similar to that set up in Nuremberg after the Second World War) has been scouted, and recourse has been made to sanctions, in preference to negotiations and conciliation.

Consequently, the professed function of the United Nations, that of the peaceful settlement of disputes, in effect, has been forsworn. The first major "success" of the United Nations after the end of the Cold War has been the conduct of *a war* against Iraq to liberate Kuwait, which has caused thousands of Iraqi and other Arab casualties, brought disaster to the immediate environment (from the burning of hundreds of oil wells), and has still left the main culprit, Saddam Hussein, in power to ravage the local Shiite and Kurdish populations. The use of military force to settle disputed issues can hardly be described as peaceful.

There is, however, no other way to enforce upon sovereign states either the rules of international law, or the resolutions of the Security Council, than by war. Economic sanctions have to be backed by force if they are to be made effective and states seeking to break them can be prevented only by military threats. So in the last resort war is the only means to which recourse can be had. If Saddam Hussein had been a private miscreant acting illegally under municipal law, he could have been arrested, tried, and dealt with according to its rules. But he is the president of a sovereign country against which no such legal action is possible. It follows that if his annexation of Kuwait as a fifth province of Iraq was to be disputed by more than words, it would have to be by military conquest.

The other significant action of the United Nations since the end of the Cold War has been to convene the Middle East peace conference; and that has been fraught throughout with disagreement between the parties and shows scant prospect of success, largely because the United Nations' authority cannot effectively be exercised against the sovereign rights of Israel, which it is, by its charter, committed to uphold; and Israel continues to be intransigent about Palestinian representation, while the Arab states demand the return of occupied territory (to which Israel refuses to agree) in return for peace. The facts that there is a strong Jewish lobby in America and that the United States is a firm ally of Israel have not been inconsiderable in preventing the United Nations from taking the same kind of action when Israel has refused to respect Security Council resolutions as it has done against Iraq and Libya.

The success of negotiations for the release of Western hostages in Lebanon, conducted with the good offices of the Secretary General of the United Nations, was the result of several factors. First, the Western governments could not negotiate directly, for they had abjured all negotiation with terrorists; so a neutral intermediary was indispensable. Second, the national interest of Iran, whose influence with the hostage holders was paramount, required better economic and diplomatic relations with the West after the withdrawal of support by the Soviet Union. It is significant that these negotiations produced little result by way of the release of Lebanese hostages (in particular Sheikh Obeid) held by Israel, whose perceived national interests lay elsewhere.

The United Nations can sponsor international conferences on the environment as well as on the settlement of disputes, and occasionally it does so, but whatever is agreed in such conventions is subject to the limitations that we have already noticed. Much the same applies to even more authoritative scientific conferences, the recommendations of which are seldom met with any very enthusiastic response by governments; and even when some deference is paid to them the action taken is usually niggardly and insufficient, as exemplified by the United States' reluctance to accept the recommendations made by the Intergovernmental Panel on Climate Change with respect to CO_2 emissions. The reason for this is that national interests are always given precedence over global needs by the governments affected, especially where industrial lobbies are strong and active. The much publicized agreement on climate change reached to boost the Earth Summit in Rio was lamentably deficient in its failure to set any date for the stabilization of CO_2 emissions, and inasmuch as it was not legally binding, it was virtually useless. The summit itself produced only nonbinding agreements, little more than pious aspirations, that have so far produced no visible effects.

At the 1992 summit meeting of the Security Council proposals were made clearly aimed at restoring some of the almost forgotten aims of the United Nations. President Mitterrand of France proposed the establishment of an international rapid deployment army to be used in cases of threatened conflict. The suggestion, which, after all, is only a reminder of what the charter originally laid down in Articles XLII–XLV, was not received by other members of the council with any great enthusiasm, and if it had been, it may have raised awkward questions. First and foremost, one might ask, how would a rapid deployment military force prevent conflict otherwise than by threatening conflict, supposing, as is necessary, that it is to be deployed against sovereign nations? Next, it should be questioned, under whose command and direction would such a force be employed? Long ago, soon after the United Nations had been founded, I suggested that the "teeth" with which its original charter was reputed to provide the organization (and which never were provided) could only be false teeth, because their provision would be at the discretion of its sovereign members, who could be forced to comply only by the means they themselves agreed to supply. I predicted that, for this reason, no international force would be forthcoming,[2] a prediction that proved to be correct. Perhaps, then, we should not be very surprised that President Mitterrand's proposal has not been endorsed, and that once again the emphasis has been given to the old (and somewhat outworn) idea of "collective security."

In this connection Boris Yeltsin proposed that the nuclear nations should cooperate in the development of space-based defenses against the use of ballistic missiles, and the merging of developments already made by Russia and the United States. Once again, his proposal was not taken up, least of all by President Bush, who had evident interest in retaining an exclusive hold on the American Strategic Defense Initiative (SDI). But if the idea had been accepted the question would remain whether such a system of space-based defense was really as purely defensive as is professed, or if it might not become an even more potent means of first-strike offense against any who could not take advantage of it. Moreover, the further question of how, and by whom, it would be controlled and used remains to be answered. The issue has since become largely academic since Congress has virtually abandoned the SDI for lack of funds.

Mr. Major declared that the United Nations should henceforth take steps to prevent situations of tension from developing into open conflict. This was its original purpose, and its charter provides the means, although seldom, if ever, has it succeeded in the past in nipping critical situations in the bud. It is not clear now how Mr. Major's demand is to be met, or what new provision he had in mind.

Various reforms of the council were adumbrated: the inclusion of Japan among its permanent members, the admission of Germany, and an Indian proposal for further changes in the permanent membership. These suggestions are all, for the present, provisional, and only the future will determine whether any of them will be implemented, or what effect, if they are, they will have on the operation and effectiveness of the international body. For the moment, their reception has been somewhat half-hearted, and what is fairly patent is that they all derive from the assertion by the nations most closely affected (Japan, India, and any others that may be similarly concerned) of their national interests and presumed rights. They would not affect the veto right of the permanent members, unless it is intended to extend it to others as well, which is hardly likely.

There does not appear to be any great prospect of significant change, therefore, in the effectiveness of the United Nations with respect to peacekeeping and the pacific settlement of disputes, apart from advantages gained from the (temporary?) rapprochement between the superpowers. But, if the ultimate threat of nuclear disruption of the environment and even of final holocaust is to be effectively countered, some greater assurance than the United Nations has hitherto offered is urgently needed and absolutely indispensable.

Undoubtedly, some of the critical situations existing around the world can be mitigated by means already at hand. It is quite conceivable that, for example, the conflict in Mozambique could be brought to an end by measures similar to those that ended the civil war in Angola, and that some mediating body might be able to bring peace to Somalia. Similarly, it is possible that the dispute and fighting in Azerbaijan over Nagorno-Karabakh could be settled by neutral observers and outside mediators. Nevertheless, many of the minor issues are closely connected with latent, or overt, power struggles between the major powers, which cannot themselves be so easily resolved.

The Yugoslav civil strife shows little chance of being pacified by the intervention of peacekeeping forces from either, or both, the European Community and the United Nations. The appeal by the president of the newly formed Republic of Bosnia-Herzegovina for external military assistance to end the civil strife in his country bodes ill for the peace of Europe. Meanwhile attempts made by the international community and its official bodies to pacify the warring factions have foundered on the intransigence of the combatants and are constantly hampered by the recognition of the main opposing parties as sovereign independent states, whose acceptance of proposed peacekeeping measures (humanitarian relief to beleaguered people and to refugees, inspection of alleged concentration camps, monitoring of the use of heavy weapons, and the like) is taken as a prior condition, and even when given is generally ineffective in practice.

It should be clearly apparent that the chief problems of maintaining world peace and of conserving the environment cannot be met except by global action and international cooperation, which is so difficult to come by that efforts to secure it seem almost always to end in frustration. Why should this be so?

The answer lies in one word: Sovereignty. Because nations are sovereign, they view their national interests as paramount, and for each these take precedence over global requirements that are seldom fully appreciated, are often controversial, and are only vaguely, if at all, recognized. Consequently, agreements are reached, when they are, only with difficulty, and they are always precarious, for reasons some of which have already been indicated. The problem is so deep-seated, and is so rarely understood or admitted, and its necessary consequences are so grave, that it deserves separate treatment in a special chapter devoted to a detailed discussion.

Notes

1. Cf. E. E. Harris, *The Survival of Political Man* (Johannesburg: Witwatersrand University Press, 1950), intro., and *Annihilation and Utopia* (London: G. Allen and Unwin, 1966), chap. 1 and appendix.
2. Harris, *The Survival of Political Man*, pp. 106f.

4

Sovereignty and Power Politics

THE AIM OF THE DISCUSSION

To guard against diversion of attention to side issues and distraction by red herrings, it would be well to state at the outset just what is the aim of this discussion—not just its primary aim, but its sole aim. Having reviewed the state of the planet and of the nations by whom it is inhabited, and having found that mankind is facing the most dire prospect of extinction from environmental catastrophe, if not from the apocalyptic ravages of nuclear war (or possibly from both), our object is to discover what feasible remedy is available to the people of the world to the ills that threaten this denouement to the history of the human race. It is clear that the measures to be adopted must be global in scope, and that nothing less will avail. It is equally clear that nothing national sovereign states can do will be sufficient and that the least that has any promise of success can be achieved only through comprehensive international action. So our central question is how this can be brought about, not just eventually in the distant future, but immediately. For deterioration of the environment has already advanced so far, and its reversal is already so precarious, that the time at our disposal is extremely limited and the urgency of the problems is acute.

SOVEREIGNTY

It is not my intention at this juncture, therefore, to discuss at any length the theory of sovereignty, which has a long history, and many versions of which have been proposed in the past. I shall not recall them now, nor any, such as may be, that are entertained at present. I have done this before in

43

The Survival of Political Man and in *Annihilation and Utopia.*[1] All that needs mention here are the salient points:

1. Every organized social system, to be effective and successful, requires the observance of laws regulating the conduct of its members. Such laws must be known, administered, interpreted, and enforced, and any disputes concerning them must be adjudicated by an impartial authority, which is paramount and whose pronouncements and decisions are final. Every such society, therefore, must be ruled by a sovereign body, be it monarch, president, assembly, or some constitutional order involving several such institutions, which legislates, promulgates, adjudicates, and enforces the law.

2. The sovereignty of such a body involves two essential features: (a) power, unchallengeable by any private person, individual or corporate; and (b) authority derivative from the consent, the approval (tacit or overt), or at least the acquiescence of the majority of its subjects. The condition of such approval is, in the long run, the service by the policies of the government of the interests of the nation, among which one of the most vital is security. These two aspects of sovereignty I have in the past called the juristic and the ethical.[2]

3. Law, to be real and effective, must be enforceable. It is not sufficient merely to pronounce and codify rules if there are no sanctions applicable when they are transgressed. However reasonable and law-abiding most people may be, they are always subject to the temptation to prefer their own advantage to that of others, there are always differences of opinion about the interpretation (and so about the requirement) of the law, and there are always those who, even if a minority, will attempt to evade or to violate the law in what they take to be their own interest, and so to hold others to ransom. Accordingly, if the law is to serve its purpose efficiently, some degree of force is needed to ensure compliance.

There can be no doubt that at the present time the independent nations of the world arrogate to themselves sovereign jurisdiction, and recognition of them by the international community consists precisely in the admission that they are sovereign nations. In this respect, their sovereignty is viewed as paramount. There is no internal authority that can rightfully challenge it, and none that can, without insurrection, resist it. Its supremacy in law is not questioned, and the hold on power of the government of the day is dependent ultimately only on its acceptance by its subjects and the adequacy of its defense against invasion by which alone it can be threatened from without. This is the firm view adopted in international law, as has been stated by Dr. H. Lauterpacht:

The sovereign State does not acknowledge a central executive above itself; it does not recognize a legislation above itself; it owes no obedience to a judge above itself.[3]

And in the judgment of the Palmas case (1928), we have the following definition:

Sovereignty in the relations between States signifies independence. Independence in regard to a portion of the globe is the right to exercise therein, to the exclusion of any other State, the functions of a State . . .

Should anybody object that these pronouncements are half a century old, we need only point to the practices of contemporary states and their attitude to any attempt to interfere in their internal affairs (for instance, China, with respect to its action in Tiananmen Square; Iraq, with respect to its annexation of Kuwait, or its treatment of its Kurdish and Shiite subjects; Israel, with respect to its treatment of Palestinians and the establishment of settlements in the occupied territories) to show that the judgments are not out of date. Such developments as the European Parliament and the European Economic Community (EEC) Commission in Brussels do not contradict them, for the submission by member states to the decisions of the community follows upon treaty arrangements, agreed by the sovereign nations concerned, and subject to such qualifications as their sovereignty demands.

SECURITY AND VITAL INTERESTS

It is obvious that the government of every state with sovereign independence will give precedence, in fact, will devote itself exclusively to the furtherance of its national interests, and, as it can do so only as long as the state remains independent, its first and overriding concern must be its means of defense against attack and aggression from foreign sources. Security, therefore, is always the paramount consideration of independent sovereign nations, and each attempts to acquire and to maintain as strong a military capability as it can. Other states are, for reasons which will presently become progressively more apparent, potential opponents, especially those closest to the home state's borders. Thus today we find Pakistan hostile to India, India hostile to China, Indonesia suspicious of Australia, and China harboring strained relations with Russia.

When wealth or population is inadequate for any state to maintain from its own resources sufficient forces for its safety, it seeks to ally itself with some stronger power, with which its interests most nearly coincide. The structure of alignments, in consequence, tends to take the form of opposing blocs, each regarding the other as a potential enemy.

THE BALANCE OF POWER

The natural consequence is a continual effort in international relations to maintain a balance of power, such that each state, or each bloc, is able to threaten the other just sufficiently to deter attack, and when any power seeks to increase its military strength and to aggrandize itself sufficiently to seem able more easily to overpower its rivals, its potential opponent immediately seeks to increase its own power to prevent this. The inevitable result is an arms race to which there is no reliable antidote. Even the persisting need merely to keep weapons up to date stimulates competition, scientific and technological advances fuel the rivalry still further, and tensions are always, in consequence, liable to rise, and crises to recur, until finally the balance is upset and the nations are engulfed in conflict.

The history of the past two centuries copiously illustrates the truth of these statements. It has been one of successive great wars, interspersed with crises, threats, and minor wars, always, in one way or another, aiming to maintain the balance of power, a balance which is constantly unstable and always threatening to break down, because one side or the other is forever seeking to gain an advantage. So Europe went from the Napoleonic Wars (to go back no farther) to the Balkan Wars, to the Crimean War and to the Franco-Prussian War, and thence to the first Great War involving most of the important nations of the world. What was called the war to end all war then proved to be no more than the curtain raiser to a fresh period of minor conflicts and crises, that eventually sparked off the Second World War. Since then, the pattern has not really changed; there have been more than 150 wars the world over since 1945, and between the superpowers and their respective allies a so-called Cold War varying from time to time in intensity. That, for reasons largely economic, has now come to an end, at least for the present, but there is by no means any reliable assurance that the general pattern will not continue.

What must not escape notice is that policies of so-called deterrence are universal and are not altered by the possession of nuclear weapons. Such policies are no other than the perennial endeavor to maintain the balance of power, each side amassing sufficient military strength to deter the other from aggression. That balance, as has been said, is always unstable and is apt to be upset not only by political changes but even by a technical breakthrough in weaponry; so deterrence is never a guarantee against the outbreak of war. If the weapons of the combatants happen to be those of widespread destruction, so much is the danger of worldwide catastrophe increased. No doubt, the threat of nuclear onslaught may make nations more reluctant to resort to force if that is avoidable, but the possession of nuclear weapons does not prevent them from using that threat in the conduct of their affairs whenever they think it necessary. That is precisely what the policy of deterrence amounts to. And no threat is credible unless there is a firm intention to carry it out. So what is called deterrence only makes the outbreak of nuclear war more probable rather than less, if resort to conventional weapons should prove insufficient to procure victory or avert defeat.

The assumption frequently made that the possession of nuclear weapons by the major powers is what has prevented the outbreak of another world war is specious. Although we have been spared that cataclysm for nearly fifty years, that is no historical precedent. Nearly a hundred years intervened between the Battle of Waterloo and the First World War, during which nobody had dreamt of nuclear weapons. Of the numerous wars that have occurred since 1945 any might have escalated into a major conflagration, and no country possessing nuclear capability will refrain from using it if it is attacked and is unable to prevail with the use of conventional weapons alone. In the sixties writers like Hermann Kahn sought to make it credible that a nuclear war could be won and survived, contradicting the assumption that a threat of nuclear retaliation would always deter a prospective aggressor; and the strategies worked out by the Pentagon in Washington contemplated preventive strikes which brought the world perilously near the fatal brink. Moreover, the technologies involved in the delivery of the weapons has become so sophisticated and sensitive that the accidental triggering of a nuclear attack has been made ever more likely, be the supposed deterrent effect what it may.

TREATIES

The validity of treaties and the assurance they might offer is profoundly affected by the sovereign independence of their signatories. Never have treaty obligations been respected beyond what the participants consider is in their national interests. The most respectable statesmen have declared that the violation of treaty requirements is justified whenever necessary to preserve the "vital interests" of the nation;[4] and the pages of history are littered with examples of wanton transgressions, of the renouncement of treaties by signatories who no longer find them advantageous, and of arbitrary interpretations of the terms of a treaty by the participants to suit their own interests. In the seventeenth century, Charles II of England, having joined an alliance with Sweden and the Netherlands in 1688, signed the secret Treaty of Dover in 1671 and joined in the following year with Louis XIV of France in a war against Holland. That was not the first such example, and since then treaties have repeatedly been decried and treated as "scraps of paper" when they became an embarrassment or a hindrance to any signatory. Kaiser Wilhelm II of Germany tore up the treaty forbidding him to invade a neutral Belgium; and Hitler's disregard of treaty obligations was notorious, in his reoccupation of the Saar, in his occupation of Czechoslovakia once he had acquired the Sudetenland (which included the natural defenses of the country) after guaranteeing its safety, and in his invasion of the Soviet Union after having signed a nonaggression pact with Stalin in 1939. Other examples are plentiful enough and would not be difficult to cite. But let these suffice.

The hallowed principle in international law: *pacta sunt servanda* thus becomes a dead letter; it always was in any case qualified by the proviso that all conventions were to be understood as holding only if "things remained the same." Nor is there any sanction that can be applied against sovereign states in cases of violation except retaliation, reprisals of some kind, or military action. Treaties are thus never a reliable hedge against war and are little more than a provisional and temporary resource for the procurement of advantage among parties whose national interests happen, for the time being, to concur. There can never be any assurance that agreements between sovereign states, even though they are reached only when the interests of the parties are served, will be observed in the future.

Although all treaties are supposed to be registered with the United Nations, that cannot guarantee that they will be observed, because the parties are always sovereign states that have absolute discretion to interpret the terms as they think fit, or to abrogate the treaty at will, and have no compunction, when they consider their sovereign interests to be threatened, about simply ignoring their acknowledged commitments, usually on some pretext alleged to be permitted by international law. Because the United Nations Charter is itself no more than a treaty, it cannot prevent these blatant aberrations from the professed norm, the more so that, like international law itself, it pronounces the sanctity of sovereign rights and is committed to uphold and to respect the sovereign independence of its members.

DISARMAMENT

The implications for disarmament of this unreliability of the sanctity of treaties are momentous. Disarmament is practicable in the circumstances we have outlined only by means of international agreements. Unilateral action, were it to be taken, would leave the country concerned vulnerable to attack by any aggressor that felt strong enough to invade it. In short, it would be exposed to the risk of losing its sovereign independence. Disarmament by states remaining sovereign and independent, therefore, can only be brought about by treaty arrangement. But conformity with treaties can never be ensured unless by military threat or action. Other forms of "pressure" are always liable to prove ineffective if they are not backed by force, and that requires the maintenance of arsenals. But if the treaty concerned is designed to limit the very instruments of applying such force, it cancels out the only means at the disposal of the parties of ensuring its observance. The natural result is that never in history had any genuine disarmament treaty been concluded until the 1980s, when Gorbachev and Reagan agreed to dispense with their intermediate ballistic missiles; and even that accord has been criticized as an agreement to do no more than forego the use of weapons already obsolete and dispensable in the strategies currently being adopted by their military advisors—as if the prospective combatants in the First World War had agreed to abolish the use of flint-locks. Disarmament treaties are, therefore, self-stultifying. If they are concluded, their observance can never be confidently anticipated, and the only available method of providing against their violation is what the treaties themselves seek to restrict or abolish.

INTERNATIONAL LAW

The insecurity of international agreements has far-reaching effects upon the relations between states. By it, international law is rendered nugatory whenever vital national interests come into play. International law has no firmer status than that of a treaty, for its foundation is no other than the Hague and Geneva conventions. Learned treatises on the subject, from Grotius to the present day, are often brilliant, ingenious, and instructive, but they give the law no force, and even when deference is made to them by the sovereign powers it is entirely conditioned by the purpose it may (or may not) serve for immediate national interests. International law, therefore, is not effective (positive) law, and is observed only when vital national interests are not infringed, or when recriprocal benefits are expected.

Moreover, the very idea of international law is a standing contradiction, because, as we have seen, sovereign nations are, by their very sovereign nature, subject to no law superior to their own (and that they can alter, or even contravene at will, if external affairs make demands at variance with those of internal policies); and it is a primary principle of international law that its sole subjects are sovereign states. Thereby it renders itself ineffective. It is not surprising, then, that its provisions are disregarded by the nations whenever they find it convenient or advantageous, and that international courts can operate only when the parties to any dispute submitted to them agree to abide by the court's decisions (which is not often); and even then, if any of the litigants decides that the verdict goes against its national interests, it will reject the final judgment. South Africa and the United States, to name only these, have at various times refused to respect the judgment of the International Court of Justice, or even to agree in advance to submit to its jurisdiction; and many disputes over what are primarily legal rights (like that between Great Britain and Argentina concerning the Falkland Islands or Islas Malvinas) so far from being submitted to the International Court of Justice, are settled in preference by resort to military action. In short, international law does not and cannot regulate the conduct of states, except when it suits them.

The authority of the United Nations suffers accordingly, for its charter too is no better than a treaty, and it lays down in the first two of its articles that it is "based on the sovereign equality of all its members." The resolutions of the Security Council are subject to the veto of any one of its permanent members, and when that has not nullified its operation, its decisions have been treated with contempt, whenever it has suited the purposes of those affected (for example, Israel, Iran, South Africa, and others). In consequence, during the Cold War period, the influence of the United Nations was reduced to insignificance, and even after that had come to an end, was defied by Saddam Hussein until a devastating war forced him to submit.

POWER POLITICS

Because of its impotence to regulate effectively the conduct of international affairs, the activities of the nations under the aegis of the United Nations is what has been described as power politics in disguise.[5] This is an apt description, for its transactions, especially in the Security Council, are simply the maneuvering of the sovereign powers in the pursuit of their national interests. Schwartzenberger has given a detailed account and analysis of such moves, and the recent events in the Gulf present a typical example, where American, British, and European interests in the supply of oil and the support of Israel demanded by the powerful Jewish lobby in the United States dictated the policies pursued by the coalition that conducted the war against Iraq. In fact, the main function of the United Nations is to provide a forum for negotiation rather than a court of appeal for the adjudication of disputes, or for the implementation of legal requirements. These negotiations are no different from what goes on habitually under the name of diplomacy in all international affairs. And that is simply power politics—to which Clausewitz referred when he declared that "war is politics carried on by other means."

The question might be raised why the original founders of the United Nations would have gone to so much trouble to constitute the organization if it could provide nothing better than common diplomacy. The answer is largely historical. The shock of the First World War induced the great powers to establish some kind of treaty arrangement that might possibly prevent the recurrence of so debilitating a conflict. President Wilson, in particular, sought to set up an international body that would direct the influence of the stronger nations to the deterrence of aggressive acts by the smaller powers such as might spark off larger conflicts, as had the tensions between Austria and Serbia in 1914. So the League of Nations was conceived and constituted. But Wilson was seen in his own country as a starry-eyed idealist, and the succeeding United States administration reverted to a more isolationist policy, refusing to join the League that had been created in large measure through the influence of its former president. Then, when in 1939 the League finally and signally failed of its purpose, critics concluded that the causes were, first, the absence of the United States from among its members, and, secondly, the League's lack of means to enforce its decisions. These were not the real causes of its failure, which was due rather to the exercise of the sovereign rights of its members.[6]

After the Second World War, a fresh determination to outlaw aggression and the resort to force in international disputes issued in the repetition of the same sort of undertaking, with strong American backing and an international military force provided by the members to give the organization "teeth" with which to enforce observance of its decisions. But these "teeth" never materialized for predictable reasons, and the veto provisions in the Security Council negated the influence of the superpowers. In truth, the states by whose agreement the charter was endorsed never intended to abjure their sovereign rights, and so could be persuaded to join nothing better than a treaty organization such as the United Nations has proved to be.

In its subordinate institutions the international organization does much valuable work, and often agreements involving peacekeeping forces are reached that are helpful in cases of local conflict (as, for example, in Cyprus); but the United Nations, as long as its members remain sovereign, while its charter commits it to uphold and respect their sovereign independence and it is powerless to interfere in their internal affairs, cannot legislate or enforce its resolutions (of whatever kind) to ensure the adoption of global measures capable of averting either planetary ecological and climatic disaster or serious threats to world peace.

The character of power politics follows from the facts and circumstances that have thus far been set out. Because states are sovereign and are therefore not subject to any superior regulation or enforcement, there is strictly no such thing as international order, but properly speaking only anarchy and disorder, in which, as Thucydides expressed it, "The question of justice arises only between equals in power, the strong do what they can and the weak suffer what they must."[7] For the balance of power is perpetually changing and unstable, treaties are unreliable, and alliances are untrustworthy. The awareness of this fact is always present, consciously or unconsciously, to the minds of politicians. They are therefore always suspicious of the policies of foreign nations and always insistent upon the need to maintain their armaments and look to their defenses. All other states are regarded, in varying degrees, as potential enemies; even present allies may, in the event of a coup, a revolution, or simply a change of government, come to be hostile. Consequently, as Hobbes has it:

> . . . in all times, Kings and Persons of Sovereign Authority, because of their independency, are in continual jealousies, and in the state and posture of Gladiators; having their weapons pointing and eyes fixed on one another; that is their Forts, Garrisons and Guns upon the Frontiers of their Kingdoms; and continual Spyes upon their neighbours; which is a posture of War.[8]

This opinion has been repeated by Spinoza[9] and Hegel,[10] and at the present time by theorists such as Hans Morgenthau;[11] and the conditions they describe persist to this day. The relations between states may thus rightly be described as power politics.

In such circumstances no independent nation can afford to neglect its defenses and the first obligation of its leaders is to look to its moat. The overriding consideration of governments and the main aim of their policies is the acquisition, or the maintenance, of power. Their motives in all international transactions are governed by strategic considerations, and, in their anxiety to secure themselves against aggression, they continually prepare for war. History throughout the past five centuries proves the truth of these contentions, but most decidedly in the last. Consistent support given by the United States administration to the white (apartheid) regime in South Africa was largely premised upon assessment of the strategic importance of the Cape of Good Hope, and similar considerations undoubtedly influenced its decisions to invade Grenada and Panama. Acquisition of colonies has always been largely for strategic reasons, and since nuclear weapons have changed the nature of warfare and made colonies more of an embarrassment than a strategic advantage, imperial nations have been much more ready and eager to grant their colonies independence. By and large, foreign and defense policies are driven simply by the requirement to maintain the power balance; this and the arms race with the recurrent tensions so engendered renders fallacious the much vaunted proverb that the best way to ensure peace is to prepare for war. So far from providing conditions in which means could be found for safeguarding the human race against nuclear war or environmental catastrophe, the present absence of order and impossibility of international regulation create the very conditions that make both of these eventualities more likely.

If this view seems, at first sight, somewhat extreme, the facts of history, past and present, are enough to confirm its truth. It does not follow, of course, that ordinary diplomacy cannot achieve anything salutary. As has already been conceded, whenever so-called vital interests are not involved, or the issues concerned are relatively minor, helpful and pacific arrangements are often made. But the crucial matters are those affecting peace and war, which inevitably involve vital interests, and global problems are not minor but impinge directly on, and frequently require restriction of, national interests, and these problems are of the utmost weight for the survival of the race. Vital national interests are almost always closely entangled with such issues, provoking the assertion of sovereign rights. Thus, like so much else, matters affecting the environment, no less than those concerning security, become the counters and playthings of power politics. It is for this reason that the solution of global problems cannot be found in the conduct of diplomacy, any more than it can be achieved by the independent action of sovereign states. Where global interests should prevail, national interests ought not to be given preference; but that is what invariably happens in transactions between sovereign states.

This being the case, what is urgently needed if mankind is to be saved from final calamity is a new world order. Recently this phrase has been on the lips of politicians and the promise of a new dispensation has been held out to the listening public. But the new world order so far offered is no more than what the United Nations, either in its present form or reformed in some respects, can provide; and we have seen strong reason to believe that the United Nations, as an association of sovereign states, cannot accomplish what is required. Some other institutional form is, therefore, essential, and careful consideration must be given to the sort of new world order that could appropriately and competently achieve the required end.

Notes

1. E. E. Harris, *The Survival of Political Man* (Johannesburg: Witwatersrand University Press, 1950), chap. 2, and *Annihilation and Utopia* (London: G. Allen and Unwin, 1966), chap. 3.
2. Cf. ibid.
3. Cf. H. Lauterpacht, *The Function of Law in the International Community* (Oxford: Clarendon Press, 1933), p. 64.
4. Cf. the public statements of prominent political figures quoted in *The Survival of Political Man*, p. 53.
5. Cf. *The Survival of Political Man*, chap. 5.
6. Cf. G. Schwarzenberger, *Power Politics*, 2nd ed. (London: Stevens and Sons Ltd., 1951), Part 2; E. E. Harris, *The Survival of Political Man*, chaps. 4, 5, and 6, and *Annihilation and Utopia*, chap. 6.
7. Thucydides, *The Peloponnesian War*, chap. 5.
8. T. Hobbes, *Leviathan* (1651; reprint, Oxford: Clarendon Press, 1909, 1929–43), chap. 13.
9. Cf. B. de Spinoza, *Tractatus Politicus*, chap. 3, §13.
10. Cf. G. W. F. Hegel, *Grundlinien der Philosophie des Rechts*, trans. by T. M. Knox as *Hegel's Philosophy of Right* (Oxford: Clarendon Press, 1942–53), §§330–50.
11. Cf. H. Morgenthau, *Politics among the Nations* (New York: Knopf, 1948–78).

5

The New World Order

Has Anything Changed?

Since the dissolution of the Soviet Union and the revolutions in the Central European countries, journalists and politicians have spoken of a new world order as already having sprung into being; but the analysis of the international situation so far given shows that nothing of the sort has really happened. There has been no change in the world order, only in the balance of power. That change, however, does offer a new opportunity for the establishment of a new world order, if only the nations can be persuaded to embark upon it. What is needed is first to decide what can be effective in remedying the urgent and desperate global ills that now beset all peoples the world over, then to consider what sort of new order is desirable and what is practicable.

Proposals for Change

It is not only now that proposals for a new world order have come to the fore. Ever since the end of the Second World War and the establishment of the United Nations, political theorists and jurists have felt that the institutions provided for the pacific settlement of disputes between nations were unsatisfactory and unable to perform their intended function. Four different types of proposal have been made that merit some consideration: (a) reform of the United Nations, (b) obligatory legal adjudication ("peace through law"), (c) the fostering and growth of an international civil society, and (d) world federalism. In this chapter we shall be mainly concerned with the first three of these proposals, and our aim will be to discover whether any of them could really deliver the promised result.

55

(A) UNITED NATIONS REFORM

Proposed reforms of the United Nations have included the enlargement of the Security Council, the abolitions of the veto by its permanent members, direct election of representatives to the General Assembly, and the removal of the present prohibition against interference in the internal affairs of members. None of these reforms, however, would materially change the international system in a way that could ensure the pacific settlement of disputes, because all of them retain intact the sovereign rights of the nations and the obligation laid down in the charter of the organization to uphold the sovereign independence of its member states. The last suggestion, in fact, is self-frustrating in that context, because sovereign states will not brook outside interference in their internal affairs, and any attempt to adopt such measures by the international body could well be viewed as a hostile act and might even be militarily resisted.

Increasing the size of the Security Council would make no significant difference, beyond satisfying the aspirations of some of the minor powers to participate in discussion and decision making. Abolition of the veto pre-rogatives of the permanent members of the council might facilitate action to some extent, but even that would be doubtful, because a great power which had been overruled could easily act to obstruct the implementation of a resolution it had opposed so as to nullify any decision. Even now, minor powers like Israel and Iraq are quite capable of defying Security Council decisions, and ignoring its resolutions. Imagine, for instance, what could have been done about the Iraqi occupation of Kuwait if the United States had not supported the decision to move against Saddam Hussein, and had been outvoted in the Security Council. Without the cooperation of the most powerful nation, no effective action could have been taken. When the United Nations was first established its founders defended the veto provi-sion on the ground that nothing could ever be accomplished unless the major powers were in agreement. But the essential point is not so much whether action could be taken at all, as what sort of action would be possible; and it is obvious that there could be no other than the application of sanctions, which, of whatever kind they might be, could be made effective only if backed by military force, or the threat of its use. No dispute can be settled peaceably if the recalcitrant disputants are sovereign nations. Kuwait could not have been liberated without war as long as a sovereign Iraq resisted. In fact, every positive and effective action authorized by the Security Council since its inauguration has involved military conflict, in Zaire, in Korea, and in the Persian Gulf.

Direct election of the members of the General Assembly would increase
the democratic character of the representation in that body, and might
improve the kind of decisions reached. But here again the question is one of
principle. What, or whom, would the delegates represent? Would they
simply be delegates of the states the people of which had elected them, or
would they represent the population itself? If the latter, how would they
relate to the ambassadors of their governments who are supposed to represent them in the Security Council? For what political party or opinion in the
country concerned would they speak? If the delegates still represent their
countries as sovereign states, no difference in principle would have been
made. If they were to be regarded as representing other constituencies, let
us suppose the majority opinion in their homelands (if that could be clearly
demarcated), could their decisions affect any positive action taken by the
Security Council, which would still be controlled by the governments in
power? The answer to the last question is almost certainly negative, and to
the earlier ones highly dubious. It is also improbable, except in special cases
(perhaps, like Iran, and not even there), that the political alignment of the
whole people of any country would be one and the same, and if, as is very
likely, it were not, the voice of its representatives in the General Assembly
and the Security Council could hardly be decisive. So the proposed reform
is unlikely to produce any useful result, and would not cure the ills to which
the international comity of nations is subject.

The principle involved, however, is even more fundamental. It concerns
the function of the assembly, as such. Is it to be authorized to legislate for
the international community, and, if so, what sort of law could it enact? As
long as the nations remain sovereign they will recognize no superior law,
and if enactments by the United Nations Assembly are to be legally binding
upon member governments, those governments can no longer claim
sovereign independence. Only if the United Nations Charter were converted into a federal constitution could any effective democratic legislative
assembly be established.

Removing the prohibition against intervention in domestic affairs would
certainly make a considerable difference to the kinds of action that the
organization could take, but would hardly make it easier to implement,
because if the state concerned did not consent, its government would almost
certainly resist the interference and would have to be coerced, again involving the use of military force.

The legal right of the United Nations to intervene in civil conflicts might
well have a salutary effect; but to resolve civil issues by means of foreign
(even though international) intervention, as the present conflict in Yugoslavia

testifies, is extremely difficult. The current impotence of the United Nations' forces in that country to defend themselves against attack is constantly frustrating all efforts either to relieve the suffering of civilians or to pacify the combatants. Agreements reached to place heavy weapons under the United Nations' supervision are not observed; and if they were, any such supervision would be relatively futile, for the monitors could not prevent, even if they could report, the use of the weapons under their surveillance. On the other hand, if the United Nations' forces were given authority to resist attack and to silence heavy weapons by returning fire, they would become involved in the conflict and might be entangled to any extent and for an unpredictable length of time in what is already intolerable warfare. Were they to succeed in their mission it could only be through long-term enforcement that would require little less than military occupa-tion, tantamount to conquest and subjection, which no Serbs, Croats, nor any other peoples are likely to stomach.

It follows that such reform of the United Nations as has been proposed could not alter the overall situation materially in any way that would satisfy contemporary needs. What is required is some effective method of outlaw-ing war, because, apart from the human misery it causes, modern warfare is always environmentally disastrous. Nor can the outbreak of war in these days be divorced from the possible use of nuclear weapons. As long as such weapons exist and are stockpiled, the imminent danger of accidental de-vastation remains, with the accompanying menace of environmental catas-trophe. That, moreover, may be caused by warfare even if no nuclear attack is contemplated, as was the case in the Gulf War. Further, the means of combating environmental deterioration, quite apart from the possibility of nuclear explosions, because they are not available within the limited juris-diction of national governments, require the conclusion of treaties; and some reliable assurance of the observance of treaties is, therefore, essential. Yet, while nations remain sovereign, no such assurance is to be had, and it cannot be provided by the United Nations, for the reasons already given. The only really effective reform, therefore, would have to abolish sovereign rights. Most people will probably react adversely to that suggestion on first consideration; but if it proves to be the only way to avoid the extinction of the race, it would be the preferable option.

(B) PEACE THROUGH LAW

The second type of world order that has been advocated, mainly by interna-tional lawyers, is that the International Court of Justice should have manda-tory jurisdiction in all disputes—that the rule of law should be made to prevail in international affairs as it does (or can be made to do) in domestic affairs. That is a consummation devoutly to be wished; but there are some crucial questions that cry out for answers.

First, a very awkward and unsatisfactory doctrine of international law as at present interpreted would have to be overcome. That is the doctrine of so-called non-justiciability of certain cases. In metropolitan law, every case is justiciable (that is to say, a binding decision can be given on any case by some court). If ever any case is regarded as non-justiciable, it is only by certain special courts designed to adjudicate special classes of litigation (as, for example, those in France which hear only cases in administrative law). There are always other courts competent to pass judgment on other matters, even if there is no provision in statute law that covers the particular situation under scrutiny, for then the judge is usually empowered to decide on grounds of equity.

In international law a case is held to be non-justiciable if any of the parties affected refuses to submit to the court, or to accept the court's jurisdiction— an exemption unheard of and altogether impermissible in domestic law. Sovereign states are entitled to withold their consent and thus to nullify the jurisdiction of the court whenever they choose. If the rule of law is to prevail, no such privilege is tolerable, yet while states remain sovereign this resistance to adjudication cannot be overruled.

Further, cases are considered non-justiciable if they concern conflicts of interest rather than "legal rights." Now, in international affairs legal rights are sovereign rights, and interests are national interests, and it is the sovereign right of every independent nation to pursue its national interests. Accordingly, conflicts of legal rights are inevitably conflicts of interest. At all events, it is virtually impossible to distinguish between the two categories in practice. So whatever a court may decide as to the justiciability of a case, any of the parties (being sovereign states) can easily decide otherwise. Once more, the doctrine of non-justiciability defeats any attempt to maintain the rule of law.

Another criterion offered to determine justiciability has been the exclusion, as non-justiciable, of cases that concern sovereign rights, and the admission, as justiciable, of those that concern only minor matters. It is clear, however, that minor matters are unlikely to upset the balance of power, or to threaten hostilities between disputants, whereas sovereign rights cover virtually any action that a state may take. Only the latter are ever likely to threaten world peace, and they are excluded from justiciability. Accordingly, this provision puts the maintenance of the rule of law altogether out of the question.

A fourth distinction between justiciability and non-justiciability is that the former includes cases that can be decided under existing rules of the law, and the latter those which are not covered by any existing rules. It is here that in the internal law of states the rules of equity become relevant. In international law, it seems, no such considerations are likely to be heeded. As there are larger gaps in the coverage of international law than in any other legal code or system, the cases ruled out by this criterion are bound to be numerous, and once more the rule of law will be defeated. It may be argued that this hiatus could easily be filled simply by ruling that where the law is defective equity should be invoked, and then to allow as justiciable cases which are now excluded. But this could be achieved only with the agreement of the subjects of the law, who are, by the provision of the law itself, sovereign states, which may well refuse to give their consent in any instance where their national interests are at risk. Nor would the obstacle to justiciability have been removed which is presented by the sovereign pre-rogative of refusing recognition of the court's jurisdiction; and it cannot be removed simply by fiat. States cannot forego their sovereign rights and remain independent, so the main problem persists.

Yet another distinction is made between cases that involve change in the existing law and those which do not, only the latter being justiciable. In no instance can any change in the law be made by the court, and if circum-stances bring states into dispute because of issues that the law does not cover, there must be some legal method of changing the law if violent conflict is to be avoided. In the international sphere, however, the only method of doing this is by agreement and the signing of a treaty. Only if the dispute had already been settled could any such agreement be reached; and if it is not settled the defective law cannot be invoked. So if the law is to be made relevant to the dispute it can only be by a means that the dispute itself rules out of consideration. The prevalence of the rule of law is the condition prior to ensuring the observance of treaties, and that is precisely what is lacking whenever the contracting parties are sovereign states.

A prior question is what law the court is to administer. Would it be international law as currently recognized? But that upholds the sovereign rights of independent states, which, as sovereign, cannot be subjected to any superior law. How then are they to be compelled to submit to the jurisdiction of the court, if they do not willingly agree to do so beforehand and to abide by its decision? If they can be so compelled only by military force, or by sanctions that are backed by military threat, the situation would not in the least have been improved. On the other hand, if the law to be administered were not international law as it is now understood, what is to be its source? How and by what authority is it to be legislated? What would be its status, other than that of a treaty, the limitations of which we have already acknowledged? In fact, if the attempt were made to persuade all states always to submit their disputes to the International Court of Justice, and if it were to succeed, it could only be by interstate agreement enshrined in a treaty. But, alas, sovereign states observe treaties only on the condition that they serve their national interests, and it is notorious that they ignore them whenever they think fit.

Again, how could the decisions of the court be enforced if any of the litigants sought to resist or to disregard them? There would be no alternative to the use of force, which, if exercised against a sovereign power, could only be the waging of war, which is just what the rule of law is designed to prevent. Peace through law, therefore, cannot be achieved unless there is some world authority to legislate, and unless the law can be enforced, not upon sovereign states (which is impracticable without threats to the peace), but upon individual persons, who can be prosecuted as they are by domestic law enforcement agencies, and compelled without excessive violence to submit.

The proposal for a new world order consisting in the demand for peace through law, then, will not serve to provide the conditions in which the human race might save itself from final destruction, unless it goes further and includes the establishment of an authority superior to what now rank as sovereign states, one capable of making and enforcing law on individuals of whatever nationality. In short, if it is to fulfil the function of maintaining the rule of law in the comity of nations, it will have to abolish state sovereignty.

(C) AN INTERNATIONAL CIVIL SOCIETY

Let us then turn to the third suggestion, which is much more subtle, and also more intricate and complex. It is based on the distinction sometimes made between the state and civil society. Our main purpose will not be well served by entering into detailed discussion of the theories of political philosophers, like Hegel and Ernest Barker,[1] who have made this distinction, important and perspicacious though they are; but some understanding of the terms is essential if we are to be able to assess the proposal of at least one contemporary writer on the subject of a new world order, namely Richard Falk.[2]

According to Falk, the prospect of a new world order rests upon the rejection of what he calls "Modernism" and the ascendancy of what he terms "Post-Modernism." He gives these names meanings different from those usually assigned to them by contemporary philosophers and literary commentators. For Falk, Modernism consists of the combination of statism, militarism, and industrialism, the exploitation of science and technology. By and large, the influence of these tendencies is (he holds) destructive. Post-Modernism, on the other hand, is constructive in his view, and is rooted in personal relations, conscientiousness, and feminization. It displays a trend against secularism and in favor of religion; it appeals to normative considerations, and reacts against and rejects the intolerable (terrorism, torture, public deception, and the like), and it includes a willingness to project into and plan for the future.

Falk is cognizant of the evils and dangers of the present world situation and he attributes many (though not all) of them to what he calls statism, a term that he does not define but which seems to refer to the working of governmental bureaucracy in the service of nationalism (national sovereignty?). He is also aware of the problem of discovering an alternative to the present dispensation. He explores at considerable length and in some detail the influences that oppose the ill effects of Modernism and the prospects they offer of a new world order. This, he believes, will emerge as the result of the efforts of people who see themselves as "pilgrim-citizens" and who do not limit their vision to the confines of the national state. They are pilgrims because they actively seek an ideal order. It is not sufficient, Falk maintains, to try to develop merely psychological attitudes without taking practical action of some sort (in the form of nonviolent protest). Concurrently, he believes, there is a developing global civil society, embodying all these features and tendencies, on the strength and efficacy of which the new order will depend.

The distinction between the state and civil society is one that has certainly some foundation in fact, yet it is also very difficult to define and maintain. The state is the familiar system of institutions exercising the legislative, executive, and judicial functions of government, and whatever pertains to their operation is usually described as political. More private social activities, associations, and movements are ascribed to the civil sphere. Falk does not follow Hegel's use of the phrase, *bürgerliche Gesellschaft*, which refers to the economic system, including craft guilds and police administration; he seems to have in mind something more like Ernest Barker's use of the term "Society."[3]

As opposed to the State, Society (for Barker) is the network of associations, coterminous with the nation, each formed spontaneously for a special purpose. Membership of these associations is optional and observance of their rules is voluntary, no other means of coercion being exercised by (or available to) them than expulsion. The State is the system of governmental institutions exercising compulsory legal control over the activities of all the members of society within the scope of its jurisdiction; that, likewise, is coterminous with the nation. So one body of people organizes its activities in two concurrent and complementary ways: voluntarily and spontaneously in Society; legally and compulsorily as the State. Normally, but not necessarily, Society is confined to the same limits as the political unit, or the nation; although frequently special societies have links with similar associations beyond the borders of their own State. What Falk envisages is a wider, global society, giving allegiance to worldwide objectives and taking transnational action.

The organizations contributing to a global civil society, in Falk's opinion, are such as Greenpeace and the international peace movements, Amnesty International, Pugwash, the Sanctuary Movement, liberation theology, and Ground Zero. Similarly, voluntarily formed associations serving normative principles, like that which prepared and circulated the Nuremberg Pledge, create a favorable moral aura. The Nuremberg Pledge commits lawyers and officials to abide by the Nuremberg Principle of responsibility—the principle, established in the trial at Nuremberg of war criminals after the Second World War, that responsibility for international crimes cannot be excused by the fact that the perpetrator was obeying orders from superior authority. Another such example is the Permanent People's Tribunal set up by citizens and legal specialists drawn from different nations, who met in Rome and Algiers in 1976 to draw attention to, and condemn, abuses committed anywhere in the world: for instance, Indonesian oppression of the people of East Timor, Turkish massacres of Armenians, U.S. aggression in Latin America, and so forth. Also, multinational "blue-ribbon" commissions like the Palme Commission on East-West security arrangements represent international effort to bypass statism.

The emergence of a global civil society is undoubtedly of the utmost importance, and the influence of the associations that Falk enumerates as contributing to it are indicative of a growing awareness that human interests in peace, justice, and social welfare transcend state boundaries. This fact, we shall discover, is fundamental to the establishment of any desirable new order. Nevertheless, Falk is compelled to admit that the results voluntary organizations have been able to produce have been disappointing and insufficient. Nonviolent civil resistance movements succeed, when they do, only if the regime against which they are directed is relatively benign. Gandhism, for example, succeeded in India against the British imperial government, because the tradition of the British Empire was democratic and its professed aim was to prepare its colonies (India especially) for eventual self-rule. It was not successful in South Africa, where the government's discriminatory policy was entrenched and there was no commitment to enfranchise the subject races. It is significant, all the same, that apartheid is now gradually succumbing as a result of outside pressures exerted by what may loosely be called the international community, even if it is a community far from united or unanimous. This is an aspect of the matter to which we shall presently return.

Religious movements, to which Falk points as contributory to the global civil society, he admits can pull in opposite directions, as when liberation theology excites opposition from the papacy. Fundamentalism can, and usually does, militate against democratic principles, and is apt to engender fanaticism and to fuel, rather than to extenuate, strife. This we have seen not only in Iran and Algeria, but even in the United States. It also opposes liberalism in religion and is a further cause of tension in consequence.

Even when contradictions of this nature are absent, the influence of the movements listed frequently proves to be limited and unrewarding, except perhaps to the relatively few individuals directly involved. The valiant attempts of Greenpeace, for example, to interfere with whaling activities by the Japanese and the Icelanders have had very limited success; but quite apart from that, their aim is to ensure the observance of a treaty already signed, which the offending countries are simply interpreting to suit their own interests, claiming that whaling for scientific purposes is permissible. Similar attempts to persuade the nations to agree to abstain from exploiting Antarctica are perpetually stymied by the pursuit of national interests on the part of the sovereign states concerned. And were they to succeed, the result would still be no better than a treaty, the observance of which would always be in jeopardy, for the reasons we have already noticed.

Valuable and important though these civil movements may be, there are other contradictions endemic in many of them. The determination to abide by the Nuremberg Principle and to ensure its wider recognition is fraught with difficulty, due entirely to the nature of both sovereignty and international law. National law in every sovereign state makes disloyalty (especially in time of war) a heinous offense. If it consists in the disobedience of military commands it can amount to treason and may be subject to the death penalty. But the Nuremberg Principle requires servants of the state and military personnel to hold themselves responsible for the effects of carrying out the orders of their superiors. If they entail the committal of war crimes, and the requirements of international law are to be respected, then national law must be broken, and the individuals concerned are placed in the intolerable position of risking self-incrimination whichever law they seek to observe. Moreover, international law is supposed to uphold the rights of sovereignty, which, in this instance, it is explicitly denying. Movements to secure the recognition of the Nuremberg Principle, in consequence, are asking those to whom they appeal to pledge to put themselves in double jeopardy—an impossibly contradictory position.

The Permanent People's Tribunal may have succeeded in giving publicity to deplorable practices, but its remedial effects have not been spectacular, and Falk admits "that its judgments cannot invoke any coercive apparatus of the state system, not even of the United Nations, and the claim of representativeness on a popular basis is always controversial and difficult to investigate."[4] Likewise, Amnesty International, a most excellent and commendable organization that does invaluable work in exposing violations of human rights, is hampered by lack of all means to bring to book the culprits it detects, who, being sovereign governments, are able to deny, or merely to brush off the accusations with impunity.

The existence of a global civil society is essential to the establishment of a new world order, and it is not without import that already talk of "the international community" has become common. International public opinion, engendered by the media throughout the world, is also proving increasingly influential on the conduct of national governments. This development is the result of a growing awareness (still rather unorganized and undirected) that people all over the world and of whatever nationality have common interests that are ultimately so vital that they should override national concerns. But these common interests are, as yet, not embodied in any institutional establishment; consequently, the beneficent influences Falk emphasizes are still rather minimal, and they are unlikely to be much more as long as the "vital interests" of national sovereign states take precedence, as at present they are bound to do, in international affairs.

All the factors so far discussed which tend towards the emergence of a global society, when they do not cancel one another out (as in the case of some religious movements), are countered and rendered ineffective by their lack of coercive force, not merely against individuals, but more especially and necessarily against state governments that wield sovereign power. Civil societies can never exert more than moral influence over their own members—and scarcely that over others who reject their norms and professed principles. The civil society in national communities is coextensive with the state, and so far as it succeeds in getting its ideals recognized, it is only the legal order of the state government that gives the accepted norms coercive effect.

If this is to come about in the international sphere there must be a corresponding legal order parallel to and coterminous with whatever global civil society effectively exists. Falk, as we saw, admitted the absence of any coercive apparatus for the Permanent People's Tribunal, as if deprecating the fact; yet he is opposed to the operation of "statism" in civil affairs. He does not seem to notice that without the coercive operation of the law, both criminal and civil, society would degenerate into anarchy and no social order could survive.

On the other hand, statism, if that means state sovereignty, is a constant impediment to the regulation of international affairs in any orderly and pacific manner, and the lack of a genuinely effective legal structure in this sphere is, in the circumstances mankind now finds itself, little short of calamitous. We have seen that, without war, or the threat of war, legal enforcement is not possible against sovereign states, but a legal system enshrined within a political constitution which itself exercised sovereign authority could be made effective. It must, however, exercise its jurisdiction over persons, for it cannot do so over states that are sovereign.

What this means is that the nations of the world will have to unite under some kind of federal constitutional structure if any global civil society is to be sustainable. Yet Falk brushes aside world federalism, without any discussion of the pros and cons, as "a failed social movement fashioned by reason and constrained by deference to the legitimacy of the existing order."[5] Why reasonableness should be regarded as a disadvantage is not apparent, and the legitimacy of the existing order is something that needs looking into (as we shall do in the next chapter). If the idea of a world federation is held to be merely academic and utopian (as it so often is), the practical conditions and requirements for a new world order cannot be disregarded.

These conditions and requirements are what we have been examining, and we have found that none of the expedients (such as they are) that have so far been recommended can be made effective. None is either practicable or sufficient. Yet, oddly enough, none of them is castigated, even by its critics, as academic or utopian. What Falk means by saying that federalism is "constrained by deference to the legitimacy of the existing order" is difficult to guess, for world federalism, so far from deferring to the legitimacy of the existing order, if that means national sovereign independence, would do away with it altogether. If all he means is that constraints are put upon the idea by the deference to sovereign independence of its opponents, then the grounds and the justification of that deference have to be investigated. We have already found that national sovereign independence is a persistent obstacle to any world order yet devised or proposed. Our next task then will be to examine the fourth option, and to consider whether the constraint alleged is either warranted or legitimate. The three proposals we have so far examined have proved unavailing and *impracticable,* and the predicament we face is urgent and insufferable because it threatens to be terminal. We are therefore constrained to reflect carefully and immediately on the one remaining, to see whether that might possibly deliver results, rather than to reject it in deference to what is impeding progress towards salvation; and we may not summarily reject it as merely theoretical, or simply distasteful, without examining the principles on which it rests, the implications embodied in it, and the prospects it may hold of practicability and help.

Notes

1. Cf. G. W. F. Hegel, *Grundlinien der Philosophie des Rechts,* trans. by T. M. Knox as *Hegel's Philosophy of Right* (Oxford: Clarendon Press, 1942–53); E. Barker, *Principles of Social and Political Theory* (Oxford: Clarendon Press, 1951), Books 1 and 2.
2. Cf. R. Falk, *Explorations at the Edge of Time: The Prospects for World Order* (Philadelphia, PA: Temple University Press, 1992).
3. Cf. Barker, *Principles of Social and Political Theory,* pp. 2ff.
4. Falk, *Explorations at the Edge of Time,* p. 94.
5. Falk, *Explorations at the Edge of Time,* p. 71.

6

Federalism

The Evil Genius and Its Exorcism

G. W. Keeton has said that national sovereignty is the evil genius in the forest of international relations[1] and we have discovered that it presents obstacles to every prospect and proposal for a new world order that has so far been examined in this study, just as it has bedeviled every attempt in the past to establish a system for the pacific settlement of disputes. How, then, are these obstacles to be circumvented, or their source to be removed?

One way of eliminating national sovereignty, of course, would be some sort of Alexandrian world conquest to bring all nations into subjection under a single imperial power—establishing a new version of the *pax Romana*. But today any such adventure is ruled out, because it entails a world war in which nuclear weapons would almost certainly be employed; for no nation that possessed them would refrain from using them if it were threatened with defeat and total subjection to a foreign invader. The result would be so catastrophic that no contestant could be victorious and the entire enterprise would be self-defeating. It could achieve only what it was designed to preempt.

It may be suggested that now, with the demise of the Soviet Union, the United States has emerged as the sole superpower, and can exert irresistible influence the world over. But although this is to some extent the case, it is not true that all other countries will meekly obey American behests. Japan and the European Community are quite strong enough to pursue their own ends, in resistance to pressures from the Western Hemisphere, nor are China or India likely to become totally subservient. At all events these and all other nations that remain independent are still sovereign, and they will continue to claim and to exercise their sovereign rights, as far as their actual military strength gives them scope. They will cooperate, if at all, only to the extent that their sovereign national interests require, and they will continue to give these precedence over global considerations.

The only practicable alternative to anarchy, on the one hand, and to one nation hegemony, on the other, is for the nations of the world freely to unite in a federation presided over by an authority legally empowered to legislate and administer genuine world law that could be enforced on individual persons without resort to military might, as no law (be it called international or what you will) can be enforced upon sovereign states. We must first consider the principles, philosophical and legal, on which any such regime could be based; then we must assess the prospect of its workability, and finally the means and conditions of its being established.

THE NECESSITY AND PROPER ROLE OF SOVEREIGNTY

Before proceeding, however, it must be noted that the evil genius to which reference has been made is not sovereignty as such, but is its exercise by national states, or states assumed to be national even when their populations are multinational, in a world which inevitably brings them into mutual relations. No state can be self-sufficient within its own borders, so the existing nations are necessarily involved in mutual intercourse which is what we know as international relations. It is in the conduct of their transactions that the claim to national sovereign independence becomes the evil genius.

A collection of sovereign states in mutual relation thus constitutes an association, but it can never form a community, because sovereign independence entails giving precedence to national interests over all others, while the defining characteristic of a community is that its members subject their own individual advantage to the demands of the common interest.

It is in the nature of the case that sovereign states should consider their national interests paramount, for every organized society involves the regulation of the conduct of its members so as to make ordered cooperation possible, and that requires the imposition upon them of laws that must be promulgated and made known, that must be impartially interpreted, and must be duly enforced upon the recalcitrant. All this implies the necessary exercise of supreme power by a ruling government with sovereign authority. The exercise of that power, however, is legitimized only if it is exerted in the common interest and as long as it sufficiently promotes the common welfare. It is proper and inevitable, therefore, that a sovereign government should regard the national interest as paramount and should act accordingly. Within the nation the common interest takes precedence, and for that very reason, in external affairs, international accommodations are subordinated to national advantage. In principle, then, the nation is a community, but the so-called comity of nations, while they remain severally sovereign, cannot be.

As essential to the existence of social order, sovereignty is legitimate and indispensable. Without such supreme authority, empowered to enforce law, anarchy would prevail and people would be in the condition described by Hobbes as the State of Nature. But in the international sphere, because states are sovereign and independent, that condition is precisely what does prevail, and that is how national sovereignty becomes an evil genius. The only way to avoid this hindrance to any really salutary international order is to internationalize sovereignty, which cannot be done except by uniting the nations in a federation.

PHILOSOPHICAL CONSIDERATIONS

The absolute supremacy of the sovereign in internal affairs is the juristic aspect of sovereignty. The requirement that it exercise its power in the common interest, what legitimizes it and gives it authority, is its ethical aspect. In the present world situation, the relation between these two features of sovereignty has become of the utmost importance and constitutes the theoretical basis for fundamental change in the international order.

There can be no doubt that the nations of the world at the present time have overpowering common interests in the conservation of the environment and in the maintenance of world peace. There is also widespread interest in the defense of human rights, and it is unquestionably desirable that they should be universally respected. As Falk has demonstrated, there is also plentiful evidence of the emergence of a world civil society drawing its consensus from an increasing realization of the importance of these common interests; and there is also a growing recognition of the existence of a world community. A community, however, as has been said, implies not only the existence of common interests, but also that they be given precedence over sectional and individual concerns. It is, then, pertinent to consider what authority is capable of defending and upholding such common interests, and is thus entitled to legislate for their advancement and to be empowered to enforce the law.

That national sovereign states are incapable of serving this purpose is now plainly apparent. So far from being able to maintain world peace, their activities are what perpetually upset the balance of power and render precarious the pacific settlement of disputes. Conservation of the environment demands urgent measures on a global scale which transcend the limits of national sovereign jurisdiction. Diplomacy and international agreement cannot be relied on to ensure the action necessary. So the national sovereign state is clearly no longer competent to secure the welfare even of the community over which it rules, for that is obviously dependent on the conservation of the planetary ecology and the maintenance of world peace, both of which are also interests common to the whole of humanity. It follows that the national state is no longer rightfully entitled to wield sovereign power. By its inability to serve the common interest it forfeits its authority and thereby its legitimacy. With this legitimacy forfeited, there is clearly no call upon anybody to pay it deference in opposition to the idea of world federalism, as Falk claims to be inevitable.

On the contrary, it is essential and urgently necessary to establish an institutional structure that can enshrine and exercise such power as is legitimized by its competence to serve the interests common to mankind as a whole, and nothing less than a world authority can do this.

LEGAL PRINCIPLES

In law, the theoretical background for any such authority is the doctrine of Natural Law, dating back to the Romans and the Medieval Church, a doctrine for the revival of which there are nowadays good grounds.[2] It was on the basis of this doctrine that Grotius initiated the idea of international law, but as that was designed to regulate the conduct of sovereign states, it inevitably falls short of what is now required. The idea is not to be despised of a Law of Nature, understood as the law of reason: namely, what prescribes the rational requirements of social living; for it is only the rational capacity of human beings that makes civilized society possible (whatever other propensities and characteristics human nature may include). It is just so far as human beings are rational by nature that they become political animals. The law of reason, therefore, inasmuch as it is the law of human nature, is indeed the Law of Nature.

But the doctrine of Natural Law has always presented difficulties, both in theory and in practice. To explore and discuss the issues in dispute would not serve our present purpose; suffice it to say that the idea is far from dead and has been resuscitated in a new form by several eminent international jurists under the guise of what goes by the name of legal monism. This is the conception of all law as belonging to one universal system, applying to the international (or better, world) community as well as to all subordinate communities included within it.

The doctrine is explored and criticized in *Annihilation and Utopia* (chap. 13), as it has been advocated variously by writers such as Leon Duguit, Paul Laband, and Georg Jellinek, and has exercised influence on the work of Harold Laski, H. Krabbe, Hans Kelsen, and Georges Scelle.[3] The argument of all these thinkers converges upon the notion of a single legal system, which, whether they admit it or not (and most of them do), implies a single sovereign legislating authority with power to enforce the law. Apart from that, as they all acknowledge (either explicitly or tacitly by implication) the law cannot be regarded as "positive" or genuine law.[4] It cannot be made effective.

The implication of the doctrine is, for the most part, clearly stated by its proponents. It is that there is one universal world community, but that it is as yet inadequately organized. It still lacks, and requires, institutional representation, which, when established, would amount to a world state, with power to legislate and enforce law upon individuals. Several of the writers (Krabbe and Scelle in particular) repudiate the idea of national sovereignty explicitly, and declare that the ideal form of international government would be federal. Perhaps the most interesting and instructive discussions of the whole question in its various ramifications are to be found in Walter Schiffer's book, *The Legal Community of Mankind* and in Philip C. Jessup's *A Modern Law of Nations.*[5]

PRACTICAL REQUIREMENTS

The crying need for the establishment of a world constitution to objectify the common interests of the world community now requires no further demonstration. The questions to be answered are simply: What conditions would make the establishment of such an authority acceptable to the peoples of the world? And how can it be brought into being?

The only feasible form of world government, and the only one that could be made acceptable to the world community, is federalism. Unitary government, concentrating all power and administrative control in the hands of a central administration would not only be too cumbersome, and, in all probability, too bureaucratic, but would also too grossly override the separate interests of the associating nationalities. Historically diverse national regions would, therefore, have to be left autonomous, so far as was permissible by the demands of their own common welfare and that of the global community; and only those issues which cannot effectively be controlled by regional authorities would have to be invested in the central authority.

OBJECTIONS AND THEIR REFUTATION

A common objection to the idea of world government is that it would be too concentrated a centralization of power and would be (or become) totalitarian and oppressive. This is, of course, a hazard for any and every form of government, and in national regimes the antidote to it is democracy and constitutional safeguards against the infringement of personal liberties. There is no obstacle to the entrenchment of similar safeguards in a world constitution, and indeed they would be a necessary condition of its acceptance by its prospective subject peoples. It should, in fact, include a bill of human and civil rights, which the world authority would be committed to respect and to protect.

Likewise, national communities are apprehensive of the submergence and loss of their national identity and traditions, which they fear may wither away unless they can be self-determining and independent. National identity, however, is no very definite conception, and the unit for which independence is being sought, when a right to national self-determination is claimed, is difficult to distinguish. None of the criteria of nationality that have been suggested apply with any exactitude to what have, in different cases, been identified as nations, whether it be common descent, common language, common religion, or common culture. In fact, national identity usually turns out to be quite literally mythical: the belief by people with a common culture in their descent from a common ancestor, for which there is no good historical evidence.[6]

The truth is that national traditions are usually hybrid, rather than exclusive to one group. They are amalgams of cultural habits and institutions derived from numerous culture contacts and combined in one societal group. Social anthropologists agree that thriving civilizations are, and always have been, those exposed to contact and interrelation with other cultural traditions, while societies which become isolated decline and become degenerate. At the same time, many nationalities that have not coincided with any independent sovereign state have remained distinct and vital. The several nationalities in the Swiss federation have retained their distinctive identities for centuries without dilution, while Jews, Kurds, Armenians, and many Asiatic nationalities have kept their heritage intact even though they have been scattered among many different states.

According to circumstances, national consciousness can work in either of

two opposite ways. It may tend towards separatism where a national group
has suffered discrimination and oppression at the hands of another dominant
nationality, as has happened to the Armenians and the Kurds, or among the
nationalities of the former Soviet Union which were subjected to a dictatorial central government. Or it may bring together into closer unity peoples
of different nationality but sharing a common culture and recognizing a
common interest, as within the European Community, and the associations
of Baltic or of Scandinavian states. A like affinity between different nations
is expressed in transnational movements such as the Pan-African and Pan-
Slavic. Where the sense of common interest is very strong, however, the
overriding force is gravitation towards union. The nearest approach to a
definite meaning for nationality would be one that applied the term to a
population with interests in common, who live under a government that
serves those interests. But then the common interest must take precedence
over any so-called right to self-determination on the part of any subordinate
groups within it.

Nor need national differences be weakened by inclusion within a federal
union. In a federal system the specific characters of nationalities are safe-
guarded by the fact that purely local concerns and the conduct of local affairs
are reserved for the provincial and regional authorities, and only those
departments of government responsible for overriding interests common to
all national groups are assigned to the central federal administration.

It is quite unlikely that the administrative systems in operation at present
in national communities would be very much affected by their unification
under a federal authority. They would lose certain departments of government responsible for such matters as, for instance, conservation of the
global balance of nature (over which, in any case, they have never had
exclusive power, and could not exercise effective control). What immediately concerns the territories over which they preside would for the
most part remain in their hands. Despite disputes and constitutional crises in
Canada, this has been true of the province of Quebec, which has always
remained predominantly French and has retained its national traditions
within the federation. The states of the Union that followed the victory of
the British American colonies in their war of independence have not lost
their local autonomy, and where, as in Puerto Rico, there is a dominant
national character, membership in the Union has not obliterated it.

More conclusive than any of these considerations, however, is the fact
that contemporary world conditions have made national independence
obsolete. No nation today is independent in any real sense. Economically
every nation is dependent on many, if not all, others to an extent far

exceeding what has always been the case in some degree. More significant yet is the fact that the health, welfare, and very survival of every nation in the world now depends on what happens and what is done in every other; for that affects the soil, the water, the air, the food supply, and the climate over the entire globe. Unless and until this common destiny of all nations is widely recognized and is reflected in political institutions, the hope of resolving the difficulties and removing the environmental perils now threatening mankind will continue to be very dim.

The main misgivings about the unification of all peoples in a world federation have now been revealed as largely groundless; and even if some risks would have to be taken by embarking upon so far-reaching a change, the disadvantages anticipated are only speculative, whereas the real and acknowledged dangers already threatening humanity are immensely greater and are vastly more formidable. It is now apparent that these dire prospects cannot be removed by any of the other expedients hitherto proposed, nor can any of the remedies presently contemplated for the deterioration of the environment succeed without universal compliance with rules legally enforced; and because only globally applied remedies can be sufficient, no such enforcement is possible under the system (or lack of it) now prevailing.

HYPOTHETICAL TRANSFORMATIONS

The existence of a world community has now become unquestionable. It is what the jurists we have cited recognize and what Falk calls the global civil society. It makes itself apparent in the activity of numerous non-government organizations (NGOs), in the response of world public opinion to violations of human rights or unjustifiable conduct on the part of ethnic groups (as, for instance, the recent behavior of the Serbs in Yugoslavia). Once this world community with the global common interests that unite it is given institutional representation in a democratic federal structure of world government, the political crises that are so frequent and so ubiquitous will either disappear or be totally transformed.

In a federation the member states will require no military forces, but only local police; military coups, like those in Burma, Thailand, and elsewhere, could not then occur. As disputes unresolved and grievances unaddressed by state governments could be submitted for settlement to the federal courts, there would be an ever ready hedge against internal unrest. Those resorting to violence of any kind could be arrested and prosecuted under federal criminal law as they are under municipal law, without the need to resort to excessive force. These conditions would eliminate the causes and provide solutions for ethnic conflicts like what we have seen in Yugoslavia. If civil strife were to break out, the control of the arms trade and of the supply of armaments in general by the federal government would effectively prevent the violence from spreading or escalating, and the world authority would be empowered legitimately to send in not only peacekeeping, but peacemaking forces. In short, the carnage and misery we have witnessed in Yugoslavia could hardly have arisen in the first place, and whatever ethnic disputes and conflicts might have taken place could easily and expeditiously have been ended and equitably settled.

The frustration hitherto experienced in dealing with international terrorism could no longer hamper those who wish to see the culprits brought to justice. There would be no sovereign regimes to shield the terrorists or to prevent their apprehension. If Libya were a member of a world federation, no Colonel Qaddafi could stand in the way of the arrest, on the warrant of a federal attorney general, of suspected criminals. Economic sanctions harmful to the welfare of an entire people would not be called for, nor any military threat. Nothing more would be needed than firm action by the federal police.

Where relief from famine and other distress is needed, it could be organized and provided without fear of obstruction by civil wars. Ethnic groups (Kurds, Armenians, or whoever) could appeal to the federal courts for the protection of their rights and could be given autonomy within the federation, without any need or pretext to fight for sovereign independence. Disputes such as those between the republics of the former Soviet Union would either never arise, as they have done over the possession of the Black Sea Fleet (which would have been abolished and replaced by a coast guard, or else internationalized under the world federal government), over the responsibility for nuclear weapons, which would have been transferred to the World Executive, or over the command of the Army of the Commonwealth, for which there would be no further use. Or they could be pacifically settled by resort to legal means.

The armed struggle that has raged over Nagorno-Karabakh need never have happened if the dispute could have been submitted to a world court, defiance of whose ruling could have been dealt with as an ordinary criminal offense committed by the individuals concerned, who could be arrested and prosecuted by the federal police without excessive force being deployed. In fact, even if the Commonwealth of Independent Republics could now agree upon a federal constitution under which they could unite, these excesses could be overcome. The main reason, it would seem, why they do not is their fear of a centralized tyranny such as the Soviets imposed; but a genuinely democratic constitution properly authorized by the people and observed by the elected officials could obviate that.

Once the political battles and entanglements are eliminated, which are generated by the relations between sovereign independent states, or communities seeking sovereign independence, the real and most pressing menaces to human survival could then be addressed without constant distraction of attention by local disputes and belligerence, and plans could be made to meet them without the need to conclude treaties between states whose good faith is never wholly reliable. The plans once made, and endorsed by the federal legislature, could be enshrined in statutes; their implementation could be backed by legal enforcement as required, and progress could be made where today valuable time is lost in wrangling and vacillation without any reliable outcome.

In a federated world the entire international prospect would be transformed. There would indeed be a new world order, one in which the political troubles and civil strife that are now plaguing the nations would have disappeared, and the most crucial and urgent problems facing the human race as a whole could be addressed with some hope of solution.

REALISTS AND UTOPIANS

Al Gore has written a book remarkable for its acute awareness of the dangers and the predicament faced by humanity at the present time, for its insights into the causes of present problems and the changes in global thinking and policy-making needed to meet them.[7] But it has one fatal defect; Gore sweeps aside the idea of world government as impracticable and undesirable, without the least consideration or apparent awareness of the massive evidence such as I have assembled here and elsewhere that none of the other options are workable. Gore himself admits that the United Nations is unlikely to be able to help significantly to extricate the world from its present conflicts of interests. He sees that what is necessary for remedies to be global is that all nations should act in concert; he calls for "agreements that obligate all nations . . ."; but he fails to explain how such obligation is to be made effective, or what sanctions, short of war, have ever been, or can ever be, brought to bear upon sovereign states, that will compel them to keep the agreements they have entered into when their national interests are at stake. Gore, while he recognizes and insists that we must fundamentally change our modes of thinking if the world is to be saved from disaster, cannot free himself from the inveterate habit of viewing (even if only tacitly) international relations in terms of national sovereignty. So he declares that, in their inability to relinquish their interest in national sovereign independence, and the freedom which is alleged to accompany it, no people will ever accept the idea of world government. In actual fact, power politics among sovereign states, with its constant threats of war and violent conflict, and its neglect of the global common interest in the balance of nature, is perhaps the paramount obstacle to real freedom in modern times. So while Gore rightly identifies the strategic goals at which we should aim, the global Marshall Plan that he offers as the solution to the world's ills is fatally flawed by the absence of any known means to induce sovereign governments to agree to it where it is not obviously to their own national advantage, and the lack of effective means of regulation and enforcement of any agreement that might (problematically) be reached.[8]

The Marshall Plan adopted in the aftermath of the Second World War was accepted and implemented, as Gore himself recognizes, for the strategic reason that America feared the Soviet Union's ability to capitalize on the economic distress and disarray in Europe. His own proposed global Marshall Plan is of a different kind and is designed to achieve different aims. It cannot be financed or directed by any one nation (although Gore clearly expects and urges the United States to take the lead), nor is its object to strengthen the strategic advantages of any one bloc—as, indeed, it should not be. He recognizes and insists that it can be carried out only with the full and determined cooperation of all or most of the nations of the world. As he says:

> . . . we must negotiate international agreements that establish global constraints on acceptable behavior but that are entered into voluntarily—albeit with the understanding that they will contain both incentives and legally valid penalties for noncompliance.[9]

He does not tell us what these penalties could be, other than economic sanctions or military threats, without which economic sanctions seldom prevail, nor does he say how they are to be made legally valid, nor does he disclose by what means agreement is to be reached on such far-reaching measures as he proposes, many of which would inevitably put strains on the national interests of the several independent states. It is already clear that the nations, especially the United States, are reluctant even to fix dates for the stabilization of CO_2 emissions, much less a global plan as comprehensive and demanding as Al Gore proposes.

The plan itself includes admirable suggestions of ways to meet current needs, none of which, however, are strikingly new, and all of which could easily have been put into operation before now. But they have not been, and we should ask why not. The technology is for the most part already available, but no significant move has yet been made to apply it. The need and its urgency is widely known, but it is not being met. Gore is entirely right to insist that it should be, and his analysis and assessment of the world situation could hardly be bettered. But he gives no indication how the obstacles are to be overcome which have hitherto prevented the proposals he makes from being adopted, or how independent sovereign nations are to be persuaded to carry them out, nor yet how to compel them to abide by their agreements if they are ever made. He confesses that without legislation his global plan would hardly be possible, yet he does not say who will legislate. No national government has wide enough jurisdiction, and if this responsibility is to fall to the United Nations, what better means than heretofore are to be found to make the resolutions of the Security Council effective? Gore is fully aware and gives ample evidence of the difficulty of getting his own country's administration to adopt the desired policies. How then does he expect them to be implemented globally? For, as we have already established, international agreements will not and cannot achieve what is necessary. Gore knows what should be done, but he rejects the one and only precondition that it ever could be.

To castigate the proposition of world federation as merely academic and utopian should thus be seen as ludicrous. What is utopian is visionary and impracticable, but that federalism as such is neither is made blatantly apparent by the existence and successful working of numerous actual federal states in the world today, notably the Swiss, the Australian, the Canadian, and the Indian, and most prominently of all, the United States of America. It is curious that writers like Al Gore should dismiss world federation as unfeasible while they recognize without hesitation the success and stability of the American Constitution, a governmental system which Gore himself admires, praises, and in which he has effectively served. In the eighteenth century there were many who castigated the idea of federalism as impracticable and undesirable—witness the arguments that Hamilton and Madison were constrained to advance to allay such fears and to recommend union—yet the United States has been a spectacular example of the practicability and resilience of federalism. World federation would, indeed, be more complex and would present greater problems of organization. But that these could not be overcome will be disproved in the following chapters.

Surely, what must be identified as utopian are those proposals which, as has been shown above, could not possibly work in an association of sovereign states, and the true visionaries are they who imagine that peace can be preserved by reliance on treaties and the good faith of national sovereign powers, which history has consistently shown to be fickle. That organizations like the League of Nations and the United Nations, whatever advantages they can provide, are incapable of preventing wars and are seldom able to pacify determined combatants has time and again become dismally apparent. That they cannot ensure the observance of treaties is equally manifest, and they certainly could not underwrite or maintain any global plan that would be adequate to save the Earth's ecology from disruption. It is, then, clearly only delusory complacency and visionary optimism that can persuade politicians and academic theorizers that contemporary problems can successfully be met through their agency. The only realistic and shrewdly practical reformers are those who advocate world federation, the one and only expedient that has any real chance of success, and one for which examples on a smaller scale are plentiful, have proved impressively and stably democratic, and are practically effective.

CONDITIONS OF FEDERATION

States are persuaded to unite under a federal government for diverse reasons. Sometimes it may be that they are jointly subject to some external threat, and seek to unite for mutual protection. In the ordinary way, a military alliance, or at most a confederation would be sufficient to meet that need, if other pressing conditions did not demand a closer union. But if external danger is considered a necessary condition for federation, it is undoubtedly one now present to the Earth as a whole. There can be no doubt that the nations of the world at the present time are under a threat more terrible and less liable to mitigation that any mere augury of military invasion. The prospect of destruction now imminent cannot be averted by any military alliance, and a confederation (under which classification the United Nations would fall) is manifestly inadequate, so the one remaining course is unification.

Another appropriate cause for federation is the interdependence of neighboring states who find that their sovereign separateness creates tensions and confusion in their mutual relations, as occurred among the newly liberated British colonies in North America after their Revolutionary War against the British Crown. This again is precisely the situation in which modern nations find themselves. They are all mutually interdependent, yet their interrelation, both economic and political, is marred by constant tensions and disputes, by threatened conflict, and fatal contradiction (as when loans from the International Monetary Fund [IMF] encourage economic policies that are environmentally destructive and saddle the poorer nations with crippling and intolerable debts, or when food surpluses build up excessively in some regions, while starvation ravages others).

The European Community is clearly in this situation, being a sort of confederation with persisting strains and difficulties, which it is seeking to overcome by uniting its members more closely. Old-fashioned ideologues like Margaret Thatcher inveigh against this trend, but she fails to distinguish between dictatorial centralized government which she fears and democratic federalism which she should welcome. Instead of fulminating against the latter, she would have done better, in her recent speech at The Hague, to urge more democratization of the community's institutions by making the commission an elected cabinet responsible to the European Parliament, and giving that elected body proper legislative powers.

The republics of the former Soviet Union are in the same condition of mutual strain and conflict, with no effective federal constitution for the so-called Commonwealth to resolve the differences and disputes between its members. The reluctance of the separate states to federate is to be attributed to the fact that they had been long held together by a dictatorial and tyrannous regime, a revival of which they would naturally deprecate. Nevertheless, the solution to many of their problems quite obviously lies in some form of more democratic federation.

Another precondition favorable to federation is that the nations uniting should previously have belonged to some other form of union, either a colonial empire or a confederation of some sort. The states that federated to form the United States of America had been in both these situations. Many, if not all, of the states of the Earth today have similarly experienced some form of looser association, first in the League of Nations and then in the United Nations. Further, in recent decades, various regional alliances and economic groupings have come into being, which might well prepare the ground for closer association.

LOGISTICS

The complex organization of a world federation would require an efficient logistical base—worldwide communications and transportation. Today the elements of such logistics are all spectacularly available. There are far swifter and longer-ranging methods of communication than existed in the North America of the late eighteenth and early nineteenth centuries, when, even before the conquest of the far west, two months had to be allowed for newly elected senators and representatives of the states of the Union to travel to Washington. Nowadays the whole Earth can be encircled in a time span measured in hours, rather than days. Radio and television put peoples of the antipodes in mutual touch by the turn of a knob, or more directly by satellite telephony. Politicians can talk to one another from points widely separated and can address millions of potential constituents scattered over thousands of miles. Debates on crucial issues can be conducted between speakers separated by oceans and can be heard and seen by audiences across continents. Information can be transmitted and publicized the world over, in any desired number of languages, and political leaders can confer together from opposite ends of the Earth. Today, in all respects except political organization, the world is a unified whole, and its peoples are potentially a single community with the weightiest interests in common.

THE OBVIOUS CONCLUSION AND WHAT OBSCURES IT

The necessary and sufficient conditions for world federation are therefore at hand, and the pressing need for an authority that can legislate measures to combat the desperate global problems facing humanity is unquestionable. All that remains to be done is to persuade the peoples of the world of the danger they seem so reluctant to acknowledge, and of the one course of action prerequisite to dealing with it, so that they will take the necessary steps to establish appropriate legislative institutions. It is not that a federal structure of international government will automatically solve all difficulties. It is only the precondition, the administrative structure, that will permit the necessary expedients to be put into practice. That it is the necessary precondition is made plain by the failure of all the other options available.

The problems are complicated and immense and they will require all the ingenuity and effort that the best minds can devote to them if they are to be solved. But what is, or should now be, clear as daylight is that no effort or ingenuity can succeed as long as national interests divert their course into the wrong channels, and sovereign governments frustrate the implementation of the best laid plans. It should likewise be obvious that diplomacy, international agreements, and treaties entered into by sovereign states, but which cannot be enforced, do not help.

Why is it that so few people nowadays are able to recognize clearly the nature of the predicament in which the race is now placed, let alone the path by which to extricate it? In part, perhaps, it is because we have become so mesmerized by the achievements of modern science that we convince ourselves of the ability of scientists to resolve the problems and provide the means of escape from the consequences of their own technology. In this we may not be altogether wrong, but scientists, however authoritative their advice may be and whatever their skills, cannot, on their own initiative, take the necessary steps to effect the remedial measures. This requires government action, and there is a prevalent failure to realize that whatever the remedies may be, they cannot be applied without legal enforcement, which is insufficient within national boundaries; and, as things now stand, no authority, other than national governments, is available beyond those limits that has the power to enact the means of application. This again is due to our preoccupation with the indispensability of national independence, a fetish devotion to which in the present age threatens our very survival.

What then should we do? How should we proceed? What may be learned from the history of past federations? Let us brush away the scales from our eyes, remove our blinkers, and consider urgently the practical steps immediately necessary.

Notes

1. Cf. G. W. Keeton, *National Sovereignty and International Order* (London: Peace Book Co., 1939).
2. Cf. E. E. Harris, *Cosmos and Theos* (Atlantic Highlands, NJ: Humanities Press, 1992), chap. 3.
3. Cf. H. Kelsen, *General Theory of Law and the State* (New York: Russell and Russell, 1961); H. Krabbe, *The Modern Idea of the State* (New York and London: D. Appleton and Co., 1922); G. Scelle, *Précis de droit des gens*, 2 vols. (Paris: Librarie du Recueil, 1932–34); H. Lauterpacht, *Private Law Sources and Analogies of International Law* (New York and London: Longmans Green, 1927), and *The Function of Law in the International Community*; Clark, G., and Sohn, L. B., *Peace through Law* (Chapel Hill, NC: University of North Carolina Press, 1944); W. Schiffer, *The Legal Community of Mankind: A Critical Analysis of the Concept of World Organization* (New York: Columbia University Press, 1954); P. C. Jessup, *A Modern Law of Nations* (New York: Macmillan, 1952); E. E. Harris, *The Survival of Political Man*, chap. 8, and *Annihilation and Utopia*, chap. 13.
4. Cf. Harris, *Annihilation and Utopia*, chaps. 3 and 13, and *Survival of Political Man*, chap. 3.
5. Cf. Schiffer, *The Legal Community of Mankind*; Jessup, *A Modern Law of Nations*.
6. For a fuller discussion of the right to national self-determination see Harris, *Annihilation and Utopia*, chap. 11.
7. Gore, *The Earth in the Balance*.
8. Cf. Gore, *The Earth in the Balance*, Part 3.
9. Gore, *The Earth in the Balance*, p. 302.

7

The Precursor

To answer the questions with which the last chapter ended, it would help to look back at the history of the foundation of the most impressive and successful of existing federations. In 1774, when resentment against the government of George III was reaching boiling point in the thirteen North American British colonies, the colonists called together the First Continental Congress to coordinate their resistance. It was no more than a convention and it produced little beyond determination to cooperate in defiance of autocratic imperial rule, and one or two high-sounding documents (like a Declaration of Rights). At the outbreak of war in the following year (May 1775) a second congress was convened, but it too was no more than a convention of delegates, without executive power.

The congress did its best to direct the War of Independence that ensued, but it was not much more than a forum for debate, with few, or no, powers from the start, which exercised less and less influence as the war continued. Mutual jealousies surfaced among the emerging states, and economic crises loomed. Monetary contribution to the running of the congress was voluntary and seldom forthcoming. Paper money was freely issued, which depreciated to worthlessness ("not worth a Continental"); individual states began issuing their own currency, which also depreciated; families became destitute and confusion rife. When the war ended, disregarding its undertakings in the congress, the legislature of Virginia independently ratified the peace treaty with England and concluded an alliance with France.

In order to stabilize the situation, in 1776 the congress appointed a committee, which drafted the Articles of Confederation that it adopted in the following year, but it was not until five years later that all the states had agreed to ratify them. Even then, as the Confederacy had no executive head and no legal means of enforcing its decisions, its members continued to pull in different directions and to ignore its ordinances. Again the states bickered over, and sometimes refused to pay, their financial contributions to the running of the congress. They quarreled over boundaries and came near to open warfare; they levied customs dues on one another's exports and entered into mutually contradictory relations with foreign powers. Once more, several began to issue paper money of their own which rapidly became worthless. The effects inflamed tempers and instigated the Shay's Rebellion in Massachusetts, which momentarily threatened to escalate into civil war. Nine of the states mustered their own navies, yet none of them could command respect abroad; Barbary pirates decimated American trade in the Mediterranean and the states were powerless to prevent them, while the disunity and disarray among them, and the weakness of the Confederacy, excited little more than contempt from Britain and older regimes. Their very existence and independence seemed threatened by anarchy and chaos.

In miniature, the situation on the American seaboard in 1786 foreshadowed the international scene of the present century, first under the League of Nations and then under the United Nations. The problems faced by the ex-colonies were similar to, if more restricted in scope than, those by which the Western nations were beset in 1919, and the whole world in 1946; although by then they had become immeasurably more menacing. A similar state of affairs is now prevailing in the former Soviet Union, and the conduct of some members of the United Nations at the present time is reminiscent of what occurred in America in 1786. But the newly established American states recognized their predicament and took the necessary step to extricate themselves, as the nations of the world have yet to do.

Virginia called a convention at Annapolis, which agreed only to meet again at Philadelphia in the following year. Those who assembled there became the Constitutional Convention, authorized solely to revise the Articles of Confederation; but the delegates were acutely aware that something more drastic was needed if the union was to become viable. So they drafted a federal constitution, which was eventually adopted as the Constitution of the United States of America under which the entire subcontinent has been governed to this day.

Let me here quote Al Gore once again:

The world as a whole has now arrived at a watershed comparable in some ways to the challenge that confronted the founders two hundred years ago. Just as the thirteen colonies faced the task of defining a framework to unite their common interests and identity, the people of all nations have begun to feel that they are part of a truly global civilization, united by common interests and concerns—among the most important of which is the rescue of our environment.[1]

But then he fails to draw the natural and obvious conclusion, that the world as a whole must now take the same step as the founding fathers of the United States then did. Why, indeed, should Gore think this appropriate for America but not for the wider global community, when he so perceptively understands the analogous situations?

The fathers of the American Constitution had to solve the problem of maintaining states' rights and, at the same time, ensuring central coordination. They had to establish on a firm basis a federal executive and a judicial system that could settle disputes between the states and enforce federal law upon individuals, as one of them, John Fiske, put it:

> When an individual defies the law, you can lock him up in jail, or levy an execution upon his property, and he is helpless as a straw on the billows of the ocean. He cannot raise a militia to protect himself. But when the law is defied by a state, it is quite otherwise. You cannot put a state into jail, nor seize its goods; you can only make war on it, and if you try that expedient you find that the state is not helpless. Its local pride and prejudices are aroused against you, and its militia will turn out in full force to uphold the infraction of law.

This neatly states the antithesis that persists even now, and is at the present time much more dangerous in its practical implications. Yet, at the same time, the states were jealous of their rights as independent states, and that aspiration had also somehow to be satisfied. The same problem faces would-be World Constitution framers today.

The Philadelphia Convention had no precedent to go upon and had to work out the solution by patient and laborious negotiation. Today there is a precedent, and better, there is an actual draft Constitution for the Federation of Earth already drawn up, which needs only the ratification of peoples and governments to become operative.

In the 1940s there was considerable interest in the idea of world government. The Second World War had left the world exhausted and many nations crippled, and the advent of atomic weapons made the prospect of any repetition of the conflagration too shattering to contemplate. The idea was ably discussed and persuasively advocated in several excellent books on the subject.[2] But neither the peacemakers nor the mass of the people seemed able to grasp the crucial issues nor the conception of world unity. In all probability the major stumbling block was the mutual opposition and internecine hostility of the two main ideologies, both of them self-styled "democracy," one liberal and the other communistic. Nationalism, however, quite independently of ideology was a potent factor; so the prospect of world government faded and the idea was castigated as visionary idealism throughout the Cold War era.

Nevertheless, several associations and societies were founded to argue and campaign for world unification, each supporting different versions of the way to attain it. One, however, decided to take positive action and to go ahead with the framing of a federal constitution for the peoples of the Earth. This was the World Constitution and Parliament Association (WCPA). It drew up an agreement in 1958 to call a World Constituent Convention and circulated it worldwide, with a request to both national governments and the people of each state to send delegates. Several thousand prominent persons signed the agreement and supported the project. In 1961 a definite call to a World Constituent Assembly was drafted and sent out, which again secured thousands of signatures, including those of the presidents and prime ministers of five countries. A first preparatory congress was held in Denver, Colorado, in 1963 repeating the call for delegates. Two years later, a second preparatory congress met at Milan, Italy (in 1965), and, in 1967, the outline of a constitution was drafted and circulated for discussion. At the same time, it was decided to plan for a Peoples' Parliament to meet concurrently with the World Constituent Assembly and a revised call attracted yet more signatories. At a third preparatory meeting, in 1967, in Geneva, Switzerland, it was decided to go ahead and convene a World Constituent Convention whether any governments participated or not; and 300 people's delegates pledged themselves to attend. At Interlaken and in Wolfach, West Germany, the convention met in August of the next year and began work on drafting a constitution.

A first draft was completed in 1973, printed, and circulated for comments, and a second session of the Constituent Convention was called for 1977. It met in Innsbruck and debated every paragraph of the draft and adopted amendments. The document was signed by 138 participants from twenty-five countries in six continents. Although no governments had sent representatives, a call was issued for ratification of the draft constitution by the nations and peoples of the Earth.

A third session of the assembly took place in Colombo, Sri Lanka, in January 1979, and issued a further appeal to national parliaments to ratify the constitution provisionally—that is, with the reservation that the draft would be reviewed and further amended if necessary. Subsequent international meetings have been held in New Delhi, New York (where a copy of the constitution was distributed to delegates to the United Nations, many of whom were also entertained by the WCPA to a luncheon, when its aims and rationale were explained), in Washington, D.C., Goa, India, Tours, France, and elsewhere; and a fourth session of the assembly took place in Troia, Portugal, in 1991, from which a new call was made for a worldwide campaign for ratification.

Meanwhile, the assembly called into being a provisional World Parliament, which has met three times, in India, England, and the United States, and has drafted and approved a number of bills dealing with world problems, including world finance, climate change, and the elimination of nuclear weapons.

None of this spectacular, professional, and devoted work, conducted over the past thirty-five years, is official, in the sense that it has any legal force, but it is obviously representative of a considerable body of opinion derived from a large number of different nations the world over. The WCPA is genuinely international, and the persons who have been active in drafting the constitution include the most eminent international lawyers and professors of law and politics, drawn from many countries. Moreover, it could all become official if ratified by a sufficient number of organizations and governments, a ratification that need not commit anybody to anything more than the general principle of world government, leaving the details to be reviewed, if necessary, and finally decided by a World Parliament properly elected as the constitution provides.

The Constitution for the Federation of Earth cannot be imposed on any nation by any means. What has been drawn up is a draft offered for approval and willing adoption by people who see the urgent need for establishing a new world order, in which genuine world law can be made and administered as the one and only means of ensuring the adoption of effective remedies for the deleterious environmental disruption now taking place, and of perpetuating a peaceful and law-abiding world community.

In 1787 the Philadelphia Convention was called only to examine the shortcomings of the Articles of Confederation. However, the delegation from South Carolina came with an almost complete draft of a federal constitution drawn up by one of its members, Charles Pinckney, who argued that amendment of the Articles of Confederation could not serve to remedy the situation in which the states then found themselves, and which, I have tried to show, was similar to that in which the world as a whole finds itself today. After spending two months in debate, the convention submitted twenty-three amendments to a five-member Committee of Detail of which the chairman was John Rutledge of South Carolina, who presented the committee with Mr. Pinckney's draft. The committee, when it reported back, presented the convention with a complete draft (Mr. Pinckney's, with some additions) for a federal Constitution of the United States of America. This is what has now been done for the Earth as a whole by the World Constitution and Parliament Association. All that is needed now is the ratification of the instrument it has produced.

The fact that the need is urgent and that time presses for the solution of the most menacing global problems makes this preparatory work especially valuable and propitious. Time need no longer be spent on working out the difficult details, or on wrangling over states' rights, or similar controversial issues. All that is now required for genuine progress is that what has so far been accomplished should be universally endorsed and that the constitution that has been drafted be adopted.

Let us examine the draft constitution[3] and consider its suitability for the purpose for which it is designed, its viability as a practical institutional form, and its probable efficacy in accomplishing the end at which we aim—namely, to stave off the threat of wholesale destruction of the planet's ecology and the consequent extinction of mankind.

Notes

1. Gore, *The Earth in the Balance*, p. 204.
2. Cf. E. Reves, *The Anatomy of Peace* (New York: Harper Bros., 1945; London: G. Allen and Unwin, 1946); C. K. Streit, *Union Now, A Proposal for an Atlantic Federal Union of the Free* (New York: Harper Bros., 1949), and *World Government or Anarchy? Our Urgent Need for World Order* (Chicago, IL: World Citizens Association, 1939); H. Wofford, *It's Up to Us: Federal World Government in Our Time* (New York: Harcourt Brace, 1946); R. B. Perry, *One World in the Making* (New York: Current Books, 1945); O. Newfang, *World Government* (New York: Barnes and Noble, 1942); L. Curtis, *The Way to Peace* (London: Oxford University Press, 1941); R. M. Hutchins, *Preliminary Draft of a World Constitution* (Chicago, IL: University of Chicago Press, 1948); and many others.
3. See Appendix, pp. 119ff.

8

The Anatomy of
World Government

ELECTORAL DIVISIONS

If a democratic world administration is to be set up, the first requirement is
the division of the Earth into electoral areas, so as to ensure equitable
representation. The draft constitution provides for distribution of voting
power by denominating five continental divisions (but not necessarily
limited to five, if at any time more should be thought desirable). These are
then divided into magna-regions, in which are grouped contiguous electoral
and administrative regions, which are again subdivided into electoral and
administrative districts.

The districts are to be the electoral units. There are not to be more than
1,000 of them and they are to be as nearly as possible equal in population.
Their boundaries are to conform (though not necessarily) as nearly as
practicable and desirable to the national boundaries presently prevailing.
One can imagine that circumstances may make it desirable for some
relatively small areas overlapping national boundaries, where the people
have national affinities or other interests in common, to be included in the
same electoral district. Or again, an ethnic group now included within
certain national boundaries along with other such groups could be included
in a different electoral district for the purpose of voting for representatives
in a world legislature, if there were no other way of equalizing constituencies. The main consideration is to make representation as fair and equal
as possible.

THE STRUCTURES OF GOVERNMENT

Clearly, the first necessity is a democratically elected legislature. Next, there must be an executive to carry out the enacted laws, with an administrative branch to apply and enforce them. There must also be a judiciary to interpret the law and to adjudicate in cases of infringement or dispute. Finally, but far from least in importance, is an ombudsmus to protect individuals and legitimate associations from maladministration, and to eradicate corruption. This is not the only feature of the constitution, although it is perhaps the most important, which provides safeguards against the abuse of power and surveillance for the maintenance of justice by government with the consent of the governed throughout the world.

The constitution, accordingly, sets up a Parliament, a Presidium with a cabinet, and an elaborate administrative system under a secretary general consisting of twenty-eight departments, with an Integrative Complex comprising six agencies to coordinate the various functions of administration and to keep Parliament and the Presidium informed of its progress.

1. THE LEGISLATURE

The Parliament is to be tricameral—a significant feature. The House of Peoples is to represent the populace voting with universal suffrage directly for delegates from each electoral district. The second house gives equitable representation to the different nationalities, members being elected or appointed as decided by each national government. To this House of Nations each nation with population of between one hundred thousand and ten million is to send one delegate, each nation with population between ten million and one hundred million will send two delegates, and nations with larger populations than one hundred million will each send three delegates. The system of representation is similar in principle to that in the United States, where the people are directly represented in the House of Representatives and the states are given equal representation in the Senate. But here more consideration is given to the proportion of population comprised in each national group. In this way a balance would be maintained between the interests of mankind as a whole and of particular national groups, without sacrificing either unduly to the other. On the one hand, national interests would not be allowed to impede measures needed to ensure world common interests, and on the other hand, nations need not fear arbitrary neglect or override of those matters of special interest to themselves. So here is the first safeguard of national freedom and self-determination within a community the common welfare of which should take precedence if the two come into conflict.

The third house, the House of Counsellors, is to consist of 200 members, ten from each of the twenty electoral and administrative regions. They are to be nominated by the convocations, students, and faculties of universities, colleges, scientific institutes, and academies within each region, and elected by the members of the other two houses, voting as representatives of each of the respective regions for its counsellors. The function of this house is to provide the other two legislative houses with expert information and advice. The House of Counsellors will not itself vote on bills before the other two houses, unless there is deadlock between them, but it may initiate legislation for submission to the other two houses, or introduce opinions or proposals into their deliberations which they must then consider and vote on. The influence of the counsellors is of great importance; their function as a nominating body is specially significant. They should be persons who have a worldview and concern for the truly common interests of all humanity. Besides being instructive and helpful in the working of the two main legislative bodies, preventing rash, ill-advised, or misinformed legislation, the third house should exercise further restraint upon possible abuse of power, or unwarranted sacrifice of special interests.

2. THE EXECUTIVE

The Presidium is not to be in the hands of any single individual, but is to consist of a committee of five, each member from a different continental division. The chair of the Presidium is to be taken by each member in annual rotation, who will for the term be designated president, the other four being vice presidents. Decisions will be taken by a majority vote of the five. The term of office for the Presidium is to be five years, running concurrently with that for members of the World Parliament, and no incumbent may serve for more than two terms. There is thus little or no danger of any personality cult or domination by one dictatorial figure, while all the main regions and divisions of peoples and nationalities of the world would be represented.

The United States Constitution is based on the principle of balance of powers between the executive, the legislature and the judiciary. In Britain, on the other hand, and many other European countries, constitutions are framed on the principle of responsible government: that is, the executive is responsible to the legislature, and judges are appointed by the executive (as in the United States). While the structure of the World Parliament, with respect to the first two houses, follows the American pattern, the relationship of the three functions of government is similar to the British, the executive being elected by the legislature, which also elects the judges, as will presently appear. The members of the Presidium are to be nominated by the House of Counsellors from among the members of the three houses of Parliament, no more than one-third being from the House of Nations or from the counsellors themselves, and elected by all three houses sitting together.

At the same time there is an element in this World Constitution resembling the American model, in that the executive is forbidden by the law of the constitution to act contrarily either to the constitution or to the enacted laws of the World Parliament. It cannot dissolve Parliament or any of its houses; nor, however, can it veto legislation properly enacted, and it may not flout the decisions of the world courts. At the same time, the World Supreme Court, with whichever of its subsidiary courts may be appropriate, has jurisdiction over issues arising from the provisions of the constitution, which would include any actions *ultra vires* by the executive branch. Here are further safeguards against authoritarianism or arbitrary rule.

There is to be an Executive Cabinet of twenty to thirty members, at least one from each of the ten world magna-regions and not more than two from any one nation. There may not be more than one member in the Executive Cabinet from any nation from which a member of the World Parliament is serving in the Presidium. Members of the cabinet will be the ministers in charge of departments and agencies of the World Administration. As thirty-four of these altogether have been designated in the constitution, the vice presidents will also rank as cabinet ministers heading specific departments or agencies. The members of the Presidium will nominate at least twice as many persons as are necessary for the rank of cabinet minister, and from the list of nominees, the three houses of Parliament sitting together will elect the cabinet. Ministerial portfolios will be assigned by the Presidium, but not more than three may be held by any one cabinet member. It is explicitly stated in the constitution that the Presidium and its cabinet are to be responsible to the World Parliament, both individually and collectively.

The powers of the World Executive are limited by the constitution, as has already been outlined, to guard against the possibility of arbitrary and dictatorial rule. Further in several articles the constitution provides for the removal from office, by an absolute majority vote of all three houses in joint session, of any member of the executive or official of the administration, for good cause (e.g., corruption, malfeasance, or abuse of power).

3. THE ADMINISTRATION

To implement world law and the policies determined by the World Executive, there are to be twenty-eight departments and six world agencies. These are listed in Section C of Article VII of the constitution and Section A of Article VIII, respectively. The six agencies are collectively called the Integrative Complex, their joint function being to coordinate the working of government, to administer its finances, and to conduct research and planning, as well as to carry out other tasks detailed in this section and in Section B of Article VIII. Each agency is to be headed by a cabinet minister and a senior administrator, together with a commission appointed by the Presidium.

One very important function that will be performed by one of the agencies (the Institute on Governmental Procedures and World Problems) will be to instruct world government personnel and delegates in the nature and interrelation of the various organs of government and to give them expert information on world problems. If properly used, this educational function, especially as relating to the world civil service, could help to eliminate bureaucratic inefficiency, one of the disadvantages feared by many opponents of world federation.

Another very significant provision appears in Section H of Article VIII, which sets up a Commission for Legislative Review to examine the laws passed by the World Parliament or adapted from presently existing international law to see that they are appropriate and serve the purposes intended, and to recommend amendment or repeal when necessary. The commission is to consist of twelve members, two elected from each of the houses of Parliament and the Presidium, from among the Collegium of World Judges and the World Ombudsmus. Here is yet another safeguard against rash, inequitable, or invasive legislation that member nations might resent, an issue taken up again more specifically in Article XIV.

The first of the agencies in the Integrative Complex is the World Civil Service Administration, the duties of which are to select suitably qualified persons for appointment to a world civil service to carry out the provisions of world law and the decisions of the Presidium and the cabinet, to define standards and devise tests for such personnel, to fix their salary scales, and to employ those appointed as required by the various executive departments and agencies. The World Civil Service Administration is to be headed by a ten-member commission as well as the appropriate cabinet minister or vice president and senior administrator. There is to be one commissioner from each of the ten world electoral and administrative magna-regions. As before, they will be nominated by the House of Counsellors, but they will be appointed by the Presidium, not elected by the World Parliament, for five-year terms, of which they may serve more than one consecutively.

4. THE JUDICIARY

In Chapter 4 (above) we observed that international law, because it lays down from the outset that its only subjects are sovereign states, renders itself impotent, because sovereignty, by definition, can be subject to no higher law. Sovereign governments submit to the judgments of the International Court of Justice only if and when they are prepared to recognize its jurisdiction, which they do only when it suits their national interests; and even then they are able, if they dislike the final decision, to repudiate their previous agreement to accept the decision of the court. International law is thus rendered ineffective and ceases to be law in anything but name and theory. In contrast, the Constitution for the Federation of Earth gives mandatory jurisdiction to a World Supreme Court in all cases arising under its provisions, and makes its decisions binding on all the parties involved.

Further, a fatal weakness of international law as it is presently conceived is that its interpretation is left to scholars, who have no political power, or to the International Court, whose rulings are unenforceable, or to the arbitrary and self-interested dictum of sovereign governments, who are supposed to be its subjects and are the parties to the disputes submitted (if they are) to its judgment. The World Supreme Court, in contrast, would be authorized by the World Constitution to interpret the laws enacted by the World Parliament, and its judgments would be final for all parties, thus providing an impartial arbiter disinterested in the issue subject to dispute.

According to the World Constitution, a Collegium of World Judges is to be established by the World Parliament, consisting of a minimum of twenty judges, which may, if occasion arises, be expanded to as many as (but no more than) sixty members. They will be nominated by the House of Counsellors and elected by majority vote of all three houses in joint session. The nominees must exceed in number two or three times that to be elected, and an equal number of judges is to be elected from each world electoral and administrative magna-region, to ensure equitable distribution and national impartiality. The qualifications for judges are laid down in Article IX, Section D, par. 9 of the constitution. They will hold office for a ten-year term, but may be re-elected for successive terms without limit. The collegium will elect a Presiding Council of World Judges, consisting of five members, one from each of the five continental divisions, who will serve for a term of five years and may not serve for more than two successive terms. One of the members of the presiding council will be designated chief justice, but no one may serve in that capacity for two successive five-year terms.

The duties of the collegium will include assigning judges to the various benches of the World Supreme Court, at least three to each, except those on constitutional issues and international disputes and the appellate bench, which are to have at least five.

The World Supreme Court set up by the constitution is initially to consist of eight benches, with more to be established if recommended by the Collegium of World Judges (Article IX, Section B). On their recommendation also, the World Parliament may combine or abolish any new benches thus established, but none of the original eight, except by amendment to the constitution. Each bench will annually choose its own presiding judge and will decide cases in specific classes, criminal, civil, constitutional, and so forth; and each, for its own class of cases, is to be the court of highest appeal, except for matters deemed to be of extraordinary public importance that are to be referred to the Superior Tribunal of the World Supreme Court consisting of the Presiding Council of World Judges together with one member of each bench named by its presiding judge.

This would establish a genuinely effective judiciary for the whole world, with mandatory jurisdiction, that can adjudicate in any cases of dispute between nations, or about human rights, or concerning infringements of world law, breach of agreements, or failure to carry out decreed measures of universal benefit. Means are to be provided for the effective enforcement of the courts' decisions, as will next appear, an indispensable condition (now so frustratingly lacking) of coping satisfactorily with world problems.

5. THE ENFORCEMENT SYSTEM

No law is really positive law, unless it is effective; that is, unless it can be enforced. For this reason the international law now in vogue is not really positive law; for it has no better status than an international treaty and cannot be enforced except (as in the case of any treaty) by military action on the part of one or more of the parties in dispute. Its subjects are sovereign states, and in no other way can a sovereign state be coerced than by defeat in war. That is why international law can never be a means of maintaining world peace. International law is in effect an agreement, or convention, a sort of contract, between states. In municipal law a contract can be enforced by the courts, but for international law there is no enforcement provision not dependent on military force.

World law as enacted by a properly constituted and democratically elected World Parliament, on the other hand, can be enforced (as is stated in Article X, Section A of the Constitution for the Federation of Earth) directly upon individuals, who are held responsible for compliance, even if they are acting as officials or agents of an autonomous national government. No problem arises in enforcing law upon individuals. They can be coerced without resort to military action, and under world law they are not put into the impossible situation, that results from applying the Nuremberg Principle in current (or possible) international practice, of being held responsible for breaches of international law while owing allegiance to a sovereign government whose laws or edicts may require action contrary to what international law lays down.

The nonmilitary character of enforcement is explicitly ordained by the World Constitution (Article X, Section A, pars. 4–6), which, at the same time, provides for the devisal of means to cope with actual or potential riots or insurrection by the World Parliament in consultation with the members of the World Judiciary and the Enforcement System. The emphasis is placed on the prevention of outbreaks of violence and the assurance of fair hearings and due process for any persons concerned (Article X, Section D).

An important question, however, now arises. Of the numerous powers of world government listed in Article IV of the constitution, the first is to prevent wars and armed conflicts among the peoples of the Earth. The second is to supervise disarmament and to prevent rearmament of the nations. Clearly this poses an immediate problem. True it is that the constitution will become effective only after full ratification, and that implies that the ratifying governments will agree to its provisions. Article XVII of the constitution stipulates that ratification carries with it an obligation to turn over to the world government all weapons of mass destruction and a commitment never to use any armed forces against other members of the Federation. But if the federating nations are armed and if they are required to disarm, there must be some way of enforcing conformity upon any that proves recalcitrant. What is it to be?

Further, suppose after the constitution has been ratified by the majority of nations some few remain outside the Federation. For argument's sake let us suppose that Israel, Iraq, South Africa, and China refused to join. These are states known or suspected to have nuclear capability, or to aspire to it. In such a situation the Federation would still be related to states claiming independence in the present conditions of power politics. If the independent countries defied world law and contravened regulations affecting world ecology there should be some way of bringing them to book. The recalci-

trant nations could not be excluded from the benefits deriving from conformity to those regulations by members of the Federation, because these
benefits are global in scope, although they could be curtailed by the failure
of the seceding nations to comply. All other sanctions, as we have seen,
imply forcible backing. It would seem necessary, therefore, that until
all peoples were willingly subject to the jurisdiction of the world government, some means of coercion and defense would temporarily have to be
held in reserve.

Apart from this hypothetical (and, indeed, improbable) eventuality, there
is the question of how to quell any possible insurrection that may occur
after federation. The framers of the constitution have recognized that
prevention is better than cure. Nevertheless, the cure must be ready at hand
and (except for nonmilitary sanctions) is not obvious from the provisions as
at present set out. Nonmilitary sanctions, as we have already insisted, are
unlikely to be successful without at least the threat of forcible backing. It is,
therefore, necessary that the Federation of Earth should have at its disposal
some sufficient force, under the control of the World Parliament and its
executive. This is a matter to which the World Constituent Assembly needs
to pay attention, as it could prove crucial for the success of the Federation.

The Enforcement System is to be headed by an Office of World Attorneys General and a Commission of Regional World Attorneys. The first of
these is to consist of five members, a world attorney general and four
associate world attorney generals. They will be nominated by the House of
Counsellors (three from each continental division) one of whom from each
division being elected by the vote of the three houses of the World Parliament sitting together. The Commission of Regional World Attorneys will
have twenty members nominated from the twenty world electoral and
administrative regions (two or three from each) from whom the World
Parliament by the usual procedure shall elect one for each region. Article X,
Section B of the constitution sets the terms of office for these officials and
defines their functions as investigation, apprehension, and arrest, prosecution of suspected lawbreakers, correctional action against the persons ac-
cused, and conflict resolution. As for judges, the constitution sets out the
required qualifications for attorneys general and regional attorneys (Article
X, Section B, no. 9).

One section of the staff of the Office of World Attorneys General and
its regional offshoots—that responsible for the apprehension of violators
of world law—is to be the World Police. It will be divided by regions,
each having a regional World Police captain appointed by the regional
world attorney, while the Office of World Attorneys General will appoint a

World Police supervisor in charge of those police activities that transcend regional boundaries. Searches and arrests will require warrants issued by one or the other of the offices of the attorneys general, and the police will be armed only with weapons sufficient and appropriate for the apprehension of individual lawbreakers. As with other officials and delegates of the world government, World Police supervisors or captains can be removed from office for good cause by the World Parliament in joint session of all three houses.

A world federation would thus be provided with an enforcement system adequate to maintain world law without resort to excessive force, without danger of war, and without the frustration of defiance by sovereign states. The work of the federal government is mostly that of civil administration, in which the enforcement of legal decisions presents little or no problem, although even in such cases the authority of the court must be upheld, if necessary by force. Provision is also made in the constitution for criminal adjudication, and this too would present no great problem, for violators can be detected, arrested by the World Police, and arraigned directly by the world attorneys general, taking action against individuals, who are powerless to resist, and who will be committed only by due process of law, in which they can be assured of legal defense and a fair and impartial judgment.

6. THE OMBUDSMUS

As defender of the public against abuse of power, discrimination, or deprivation of rights, the constitution sets up a council of five world ombudsmen, one of whom is to be the principal world ombudsman, and the other four are to be associate world ombudsmen. They are to be appointed by the same procedure as for other officials, one from each continental division, and are to be assisted by the Commission of World Advocates of twenty members nominated by the council from the twenty world electoral and administrative regions. The principal office of the World Ombudsmus will be located at the seat of the world government and there will be an office in each of the regions in parallel with the offices of the world attorneys general. Each regional office is to be headed by a world advocate and supervised by an associate world ombudsman. The ombudsmen and advocates will be qualified lawyers with at least five years of legal experience.

The ombudsmen will be the watchdogs to ensure the welfare of all peoples, on the alert for perils from technical innovations and environmental disturbances. They will also receive and pursue complaints from citizens about any misconduct or abuse of authority, or neglect of duty, by world civil servants or other world government officials. They will maintain surveillance over human and state rights; see that they are protected and defended by the world courts, initiating litigation when deemed necessary; and they will keep watch over the functioning of departments, agencies, and commissions of government in all areas, to see that they are properly and efficiently executed. They will also report to the World Parliament and Presidium annually on the activities of government and make recommendations for improvements that need legislation.

A World Ombudsmus is an obvious necessity if justice is universally to be done, and to be seen to be done. It is equally a necessary safeguard against official misconduct, abuse of powers, and arbitrary action on the part of government agencies. The provision of this protection of citizens and social groups against the violation of their legitimate rights is a strong reason for commendation of the constitution and a solid reassurance for any who may still have misgivings about the need for and efficacy of world government.

BILL OF RIGHTS

Having laid out the structure and composition of the institutions of world government, the constitution enunciates the rights universal to all people, legal, civil, political, intellectual, human, and personal. They cover the rights to protection of the law against discrimination of every kind: rights of equality before the law, of habeas corpus; rights to personal privacy, to family planning, to safety from threats to the peace, and to property free from arbitrary seizure; rights to freedom of travel, to freedom from military conscription; rights to protection from mental or physical violence, torture, duress, arbitrary arrest, detention, and cruel or unusual punishment; rights to protection from slavery, peonage, and conscription of labor; rights to freedom of conscience, of speech, expression, and publication; rights of assembly, peaceful demonstration and petition, freedom to organize politically, to campaign, and to vote; and rights to religious, intellectual, and academic freedom.

This list of common rights is set out in Article XII, and some critics contend that they should be given more prominence, say, in the Preamble or in the opening articles. But that would be to put the cart before the horse. It is not realistic to declare the sanctity of universal rights before any authority with power to protect them is properly constituted. The Charter of Human Rights was approved by the United Nations almost half a century ago, yet to this day there are nations that have not signed it and many more that constantly and flagrantly flout its principles. It has amounted to little more than a pious gesture, valuable only for the indication it gives of a general recognition of what ought to be, without any assurance that it will be. The violators are all sovereign governments, upon whom no effective compulsion can be imposed, and against whom, for the most part, nonmilitary sanctions have either not been invoked, or have been ineffective. In a world federation violators could always be identified as individuals and brought to book, could be prosecuted and punished as common criminals, by a government that has received its authority by popular consent and election to exercise power that no individual can resist, yet does not involve the use of excessive force. Under such conditions rights can be protected, can be legally and practically ensured; so the conditions must first be established before the definition of rights can have practical significance.

The draft Constitution for the Federation of Earth does not stop at enshrining common civil, political, personal, and human rights under legal protection; it goes on to propose further aims and define further freedoms as directive principles for world government. The next article declares that the world authority will impose an obligation on all subordinate administrative authorities to pursue every reasonable means to actualize rights to full employment with adequate remuneration, freedom of choice of vocation, unrestricted access to legitimate information and acquired knowledge, free public education, free health services, adequate housing, adequate food and water supplies, social security, sufficient leisure, protection against hazards of technical innovations and against ecological disruption, and the right to the discovery and use of alternative energy sources. It also sets up as mandatory goals the maintenance of cultural diversity, the decentralization of administration, and the freedom of cultural minorities to self-determination. Once again, there is assurance and protection for national traditions and cultural self-identity. The constitution, further, envisages universal freedom of migration, and the protection of, and provision for, refugees (for example, from natural disasters), as well as the abolition of the death penalty.

Clear as it is from all that has gone before that local communities and national identities are to be preserved and protected under world government, the draft constitution goes further and leaves the matter in no possible doubt, by stating additional safeguards in Article XIV, to ensure that the legislation and legal procedures, the public acts and records, of member nations shall be respected, so long as they are consistent with the provisions of the World Constitution. It assures freedom of choice within member nations to determine their own internal political, economic, and social systems consistent with the rights above set out. It grants rights of asylum to persons (if any) fleeing from oppression in countries not yet within the Federation; and, within limits, it grants leave to any persons wishing to secede from the Federation to do so. (This last provision seems somewhat unnecessary and, perhaps, otiose; for it is hardly conceivable that anybody or any group of people would wish to escape from the security and freedoms assured by the World Constitution. However, the presence in the article of this provision can but serve to increase the confidence of any still hesitant about its liberality.) Finally, in Section B, it is plainly stated that all powers not delegated to the world federal government are to be reserved to the nations entering the Federation. Nothing could be more explicit or unambiguous.

GEOGRAPHICAL DISTRIBUTION OF SEATS OF GOVERNMENT

Twenty federal zones are to be distinguished in which the various organs of world government are to be located, first within the five continental divisions, but later as the needs and resources of the administration dictate. The precise divisions are to be determined by the World Parliament. In each zone, a world capital is to be established, one of which will be designated the primary world capital, where the primary seats of the several organs of world government will be situated, and the other four will be secondary world capitals, where other major seats of government will reside. Proposals for zones and capitals will be made by the Presidium, and decided from among these proposals by a simple majority vote of the three houses of the World Parliament in joint session. The Presidium and the cabinet will then propose which of the five capitals shall be primary, and the choice again made by Parliament in the same manner. Sessions of the World Parliament may be held, if it so decides, in rotation in each of the world capitals. Relocations of zones or capitals will require a two-thirds majority of the three houses sitting conjointly, and additional zones may be established by the procedure already laid down. These are simply workaday provisions necessary for obvious practical purposes.

WORLD TERRITORY AND EXTERNAL RELATIONS

The framers of the World Constitution have envisaged its coming into operation by stages, not all of the present sovereign states joining the Federation simultaneously. This halfway stage, however, can only be temporary (and should be as brief as possible); because until world government has universal jurisdiction the primary purpose that it sets out to achieve cannot be realized. The Earth's ecology is a single system and its balance can be upset by practices in any one area so as to affect all others. The hydro-sphere is a single system and the biological community by which it is inhabited is indivisible. Likewise the atmosphere is changed as a whole by any excessive gaseous emissions anywhere in the world. It follows that any independent sovereign nation of any considerable size may fatally hamper whatever measures are taken to protect the environment by a world federal government. Accordingly, to attain its goals it must have universal jurisdic-tion, and that means that it must be authorized to enforce its law through-out the entire world. As it could not do so upon an independent state without the use of military force, and as war has a disastrous effect on people, economies, and ecological systems, the objects of the entire project can be defeated by one recalcitrant external sovereign government. With this caveat we may note the provisions of Article XVI and what follows.

Section A of Article XVI designates as world territory those areas of the Earth not under the jurisdiction of existing nations at the time of the formation of the Federation of Earth, and also the Moon, to be administered by the World Executive as determined by the World Parliament. It is to include all seas and oceans, together with seabeds and their resources more than twenty kilometers offshore, excepting inland seas under traditional national ownership. It will also include vital straits, channels, and canals, the Earth's atmosphere more than one kilometer above the general land surface, man-made satellites, any unclaimed islands or atolls, and any independent countries that choose the status of world territory. Such assignation is entirely reasonable and (once the constitution is operative) legitimate. More questionable, unless all independent nations have ratified the World Constitution, is the inclusion of colonies (presumably of existing sovereign states) and disputed lands, which may choose that status, and nonindependent territories under United Nations mandate. If a sovereign state which claimed them had not ratified the constitution, there would be no feasible way of implementing the status of world territory in their case, as long as that state prevented their transfer to the Federation. Paragraph 3 of the same section stipulates that the population of any world territory not designated a world federal zone may elect (by plebiscite) to become a self-governing member of the World Federation, either singly or in combi-nation with other such territories or existing self-governing members.

The next section brings all exploration of outer space under the exclusive control of the world government, and undertakes that the World Federation shall maintain peaceful relations with any inhabitants who may be dis-covered on any other celestial body. So far so good; but it also states that the world government shall maintain external relations, as directed by the world Presidium instructed by the World Parliament, with nations which have not joined the Federation of Earth, and that treaties with such nations shall be negotiated by the Presidium and ratified by majority vote of the three houses of Parliament. No mention is made of how the sanctity of such treaties is to be ensured, and, for reasons already set out, if such external relations were not to be merely provisional and their duration was not very short, this provision could prove to be an Achilles' heel for the whole undertaking. To avoid this weakness and to ensure the primary aim of the World Federation, ratification of its constitution will have to be widespread and immediate, an objective to be addressed in the following chapter.

RATIFICATION

The means, conditions, and procedures for ratification are set out in Article XVII, discussion of which may therefore be postponed until we consider the whole of that question. Three stages of implementaion are foreseen, the first when the constitution has been ratified by twenty-five nations each with a population of over 100,000, or by ten nations with more than 100,000 plus ratification by popular referendum within a minimum of fifty additonal world electoral and administrative districts, or simply by popular vote within at least 100 such electoral districts. The second operative stage will be when the constitution is ratified by 50 percent of the nations of the Earth, or by direct referendum, provided that 50 percent of the Earth's population is included. The final and full operative stage will be reached when 80 percent of the nations, or 90 percent of the population of the Earth has ratified the constitution.

It thus becomes apparent that the constitution is offered for free and democratic approval by the peoples of the Earth. There is no suggestion that it be imposed upon any nation without its consent, and no attempt is being made (or could be made) to foist it upon any association that did not recognize and accept its necessity and the wisdom of its provisions. The keynote of the whole concept of world federation and of this draft constitution is freedom; and democratic choice of representatives and free decision on forms of government are its aims and the medium of its operation.

AMENDMENTS

Article XVIII lays down the procedure for amendments, which, during preliminary operative stages, may be by popular petition or by a simple majority of any house of the World Parliament, but shall require a two-thirds majority of each of the three houses voting separately when the constitution is fully in force. If amendments are proposed by popular petition the House of the Peoples will be required to approve it by a majority vote before it is submitted for passage by a two-thirds majority of all three houses. It is also laid down that the members of the World Parliament shall meet periodical-ly, at twenty-year intervals, in a special session to serve as a Constituent Assembly to review the constitution and propose desirable amendments for action as prescribed. In short, ratification does not commit people finally to every detail, as changes can be made by recognized legitimate procedures thereafter.

PROVISIONAL WORLD GOVERNMENT

The last three articles are concerned with the establishment and activities of a provisional world government for the preliminary operative stages, in which the work already done by the provisional World Parliament can be confirmed and continued by the officially constituted World Parliament once it is fully operative. This provisional Parliament has drafted and approved a number of admirable bills dealing with the climate crisis, with world finance and credit systems, disarmament, and environmental protection, all of which remain to be enacted by a properly established world legislature.

ADDITIONAL FEATURES

Other points of interest and import are in Article IV, which defines the powers of world government. Particular mention is made of control of population growth in relation to the life-support capacities of the Earth, as well as the regulation of agricultural methods, crop management, and soil conservation, along with the conservation and distribution of transnational water supplies. Supranational trade and industry is also to be brought under the control and regulation of the world body, which would supervise the operation of corporations and cartels. Energy production and the discovery and use of renewable energy sources would also be brought under its jurisdiction, and ways would be sought to reduce and safely to dispose of waste of all kinds. Finally the article includes the power to organize and deploy a nonmilitary world service corps to carry out projects designed to enhance human welfare.

In this way the conditions would be created that make it feasible to tackle all the world's major social and ecological problems, to find solutions, and to legislate on measures that would ensure their implementation. No other suggested procedures can give any such assurance, and resolute action that is so urgently needed and is not now being taken could be expected and could go forward, implemented by a democratically elected government and a properly authorized and enforcible law.

It should now be unquestionably apparent that world government offers no threats to liberty or repression of national identity and tradition; that it is unlikely to be unduly unwieldy, bureaucratic, or cumbersome; and that it provides sufficient safeguards against all these dangers, while it offers the one and only hope of salvation from current problems and impending disasters.

9

Campaign
for Ratification!

REFERENDA AND SOVEREIGN INDEPENDENCE

The draft constitution recognizes for the purpose of ratification the majority
votes in referenda organized and conducted by the provisional World Parliament. Essentially and in principle it is only the will of the people that, in
the last resort, can legitimize any government; so this procedure is entirely
correct. But until the constitution is fully operative, which can only be *after*
ratification, the provisional World Parliament has no official status and its
decisions can have no legal force. If, therefore, the sovereign governments
to which the people voting are subject are unwilling to heed the result of
any such referendum, no effective ratification will be forthcoming; although
the popular vote could give such governments powerful notice of the
wishes of its constituents. The only significant acts of ratification would be
those made by the established governments themselves. If they are democratic regimes this can be brought about by the election to the legislatures
and executives of representatives supporting world government, and not
really in any other way. If the regime is not democratic, it can be moved to
ratify only under unusual pressures from among the populace (much in the
same way as the Communist dictatorships of Central Europe were forced to
step down in the 1980s). There is, however, no evidence, as yet, of any
active political parties agitating for world federation, nor any popular
movements campaigning for ratification of the draft constitution. Accordingly, strenuous and immediate efforts must be mounted to persuade the
mass of the people of the need to establish a world government and to put
pressure on their leaders to endorse the constitution.

MOUNTING THE CAMPAIGN

As the matter has now become extremely urgent, it is essential that a vigorous worldwide popular campaign be mounted for the ratification of the Constitution for the Federation of Earth. The World Constitution and Parliament Association has announced a campaign of this sort enlisting several hundred organizations to work, under the coordination of a Global Ratification and Elections Network, to persuade national governments, parliaments, and peoples of the need to federate. This body should be given all possible encouragement, and its activities merit every contrivable support. But, so far the results do not seem to have been very significant. There has been no evidence of the existence of the campaign in the media. The response to appeals for funding has been miniscule, and the idea is being ignored in domestic and international politics, if not actually decried and vehemently rejected by leading figures (like Al Gore).

THE RACE AGAINST TIME

Meanwhile, the temperature of the water is rising apace, in which the frog is swimming, while it seems to be sinking into the predicted torpor. A new report by an international group of scientists has just announced that global warming is likely within the next half-century to increase the number of people facing starvation (already in the billions) by one-third. If humanity is to be saved from speedy and inevitable extinction through the destruction of the world's ecosystem, from which neither the action of national sovereign states, nor agreements between them (as I have shown in earlier chapters) can rescue it, urgent efforts must be made to get people to realize both the plight in which the human race is now embroiled and the only means of extricating themselves. This book is one such effort.

Every organization working for nuclear disarmament and for world peace, or for conservation of the environment, or for the preservation of wildlife, or for the protection of people against the violation of human rights, or for the prevention of starvation in Africa and elsewhere, must include in their programs united support for world federation, because without it none of them can achieve its professed aim; and they must all mobilize their resources behind the campaign for ratification of the World Constitution already in draft and presently at hand.

THE MISSING BUT INDISPENSABLE FACTOR

The peace movements and the Campaign for Nuclear Disarmament (CND) have been active and growing ever since the end of the Second World War.

The reasons motivating their campaign are sound and compelling. The appalling threat, not merely of devastation and suffering, but of total disruption of the planet's ecology, posed by the possibility of nuclear war is widely admitted. The immorality of using the threat of nuclear attack or reprisal as a "bargaining counter" in foreign affairs and as an assumed deterrent is obvious, even if its futility is not recognized. The enormous and deleterious cost of the arms race, even now when it is being reduced after the end of the Cold War, at a time when millions are faced with starvation in the Third World, is as illogical as it is morally indefensible.

Nevertheless, these powerful reasons against nuclear armaments have had little or no influence upon governments, or their electorates; and peace movements, even while they have grown and have recruited many supporters, have had little or no effect on policies. Political parties supporting nuclear disarmament are still seldom returned to power, and when they are, as in New Zealand, the implementation of their policy creates international difficulties with neighboring and allied countries, who retain nuclear arms, and this nullifies the effects of their more pacific intentions. Meanwhile, peace demonstrators and antinuclear protestors have been treated by officialdom in many Western countries as if they were criminals and traitors and have been unjustly defamed, without evidence, as subversive.

The cause of this misappraisal and failure should now be obvious. It is the fact that sovereign nations in a world of power politics are constrained to depend on their own armaments and those of their allies to defend their independence, and are bound constantly to strive to maintain a balance of power that is as constantly breaking down. Accordingly, any proposal that they should disarm unilaterally is automatically seen as an act of subversion and its advocates as disloyal. Those that support multilateral disarmament are more easily tolerated, but we have explained the futility of trying to conclude a genuine disarmament treaty, observance of which can only be assured by use of the arms the parties are undertaking to forgo. Until these obstacles to peace and disarmament are surmounted, therefore, the peace movements can only beat their heads against a stone wall, and the obstacles can be surmounted only by world federation. The Campaign for Nuclear Disarmament can never succeed until it also becomes a campaign for the ratification of the Constitution for the Federation of Earth.

The Worldwatch Institute does unrivaled service to humanity in monitoring threats to the environment and issuing warnings about destructive practices in every quarter, but Worldwatch cannot implement the remedies it advocates by its own activity or on its own authority. It can advise governments and the United Nations; but the first will do nothing that does not accord with their national interests, as they see them, whether economic or political, and will be more swayed by the lobbying of multinational corporations pursuing profits and dividends before planetary safety; the second may convene impressive-looking conferences (in Rio, or elsewhere), but the agreements they will reach (if any) are likely to be for action too dilatory and too niggardly. These agreements, moreover, are such that conformity to their prescriptions cannot be guaranteed or enforced; for the participants are all sovereign states that can be coerced only by the threat of military action. There is no way to overcome these frustrations other than world federation; so, if Worldwatch is ever to achieve its aim of saving the ecology of the planet, it must advocate and support the campaign for ratification of the Constitution for the Federation of Earth.

The World Wildlife Fund is pursuing a most important and necessary end. The identification and protection of endangered species is vital at the present time, not only for the rescue of creatures in peril of extinction, but also for the welfare and the means of survival of humankind itself. The loss of medicinal herbs, food sources, scientific data, and creatures of rare beauty is deeply to be deplored, and will eventually have execrable consequences for mankind. But the World Wildlife Fund is in no better position than Worldwatch to instigate the global schemes essential to protect and conserve the species whose safety it seeks to ensure, because even those national governments willing to take appropriate action cannot legislate for regions beyond their own borders, within which the species are seldom confined, and action taken by one state will prove totally inadequate if it is frustrated by neglect or counteraction in another. What is needed is world legislation, by an authority with global jurisdiction, legislation assured of enforcement—and that is possible only under a world government. The World Wildlife Fund, therefore, must spend some of its resources on advertising and promoting the campaign for ratification of the Constitution for the Federation of Earth if it is ever to get adequate action taken to attain its objectives.

Greenpeace has taken spectacular and courageous action all over the world to protest against practices harmful to living species and to the environment: to try to prevent excessive whaling, often forbidden by international agreement, to obstruct nuclear testing in the Pacific by the French, to whose state-organized terrorism they lost their ship *Rainbow Warrior*, to publicize and to campaign for a treaty preserving Antarctica from exploitation. Members of the organization have risked their lives in many of these ventures, and one life was lost in the explosion that sank the *Rainbow Warrior*. These people are truly the soldiers of peace and champions of conservation. But for all their valor they seldom succeed. If the French government has for the moment suspended nuclear testing, it is not because of Greenpeace, but as a domestic election tactic. The Japanese still kill whales on the dubious pretext of scientific research, and Iceland is still recalcitrant. No Antarctic treaty has yet been concluded to reserve it securely from industrial exploitation, and if one were to be, its sanctity and its observance would always be precarious in the face of the national interests of the signatories and the predatory machinations of military-industrial complexes. To succeed, Greenpeace should change its objectives from treaties to world law, and should advocate a world legislature with authority and power to maintain the provisions of that law. It will not attain its ends unless it joins forces with other nongovernmental organizations and with the World Constitution and Parliament Association in a campaign for the ratification of the World Constitution. The provisional World Parliament has already accepted the same goals as Greenpeace and has already drafted legislation to accomplish them. All that is lacking is the ratification of the constitution that will enact the bills already approved and give them the force of law.

One of the most respected and effective charitable organizations in Britain is Oxfam, active throughout the world in combating famine and distress, whether it is caused by civil wars, crop failures, or other man-made and natural disasters. Oxfam has fund-raising shops throughout Britain, which, by selling produce from the Third World, help the poorer economies at the same time as they raise funds for the relief of the hungry and deprived. There are few more admirable charities and none more worthy of support. But Oxfam cannot prevent or stop the wars that cause the distress it does so much to relieve; it can do nothing to check the creeping desertification that advances with climate change and global warming, driving out millions of subsistence farmers to exhaust richer soils and spread starvation further afield. Oxfam can treat the symptoms but cannot address the causes of the troubles it seeks to abate. Actions by national governments are equally inadequate to remove those causes, and international agreements have not done so, and cannot do so without reliable means of enforcement. The goals of Oxfam are already included among the directive principles set out in the Constitution for the Federation of Earth, and only an authority with global jurisdiction could effectively legislate to attain them. Although Oxfam is today doing magnificent and admirable work that all compassionate people are bound to support, the only satisfactory cure for the ills that it is combating is world federation; so it too should include among its activities support and publicity for the campaign for ratification of the World Constitution.

Amnesty International keeps watch over governments the world over to monitor their observance of human rights. It reports the many violations of the charter, and draws attention to the most flagrant excesses. Imprisonment without trial, maltreatment of prisoners, torture, political and religious persecution, and punishment without due process of law are all quarry for its ubiquitous search and vigilance. It publishes periodical reports of malpractices and makes protests to the United Nations and to delinquent executives in the offending nations. Such publicity may do much to influence world public opinion, and may prompt deprecatory resolutions from the United Nations Assembly and Security Council. It rarely, if ever, does more. The offending parties almost invariably, if they take any notice at all, declare the Amnesty report to be false, exaggerated, or lacking in evidence. Other nations do not take strong action unless their "vital" national interest compel them to do so. As we said earlier, the Charter of Human Rights is more an expression of things hoped for than the prescription of action to be universally enforced. Amnesty International has no powers, nor even any legal status, so its valuable efforts are perpetually frustrated by the inaction and neglect of the major democracies as much as by the contempt and reneging of the offending governments.

The human rights that Amnesty espouses and defends and the surveillance that Amnesty so skillfully maintains are all embodied in the World Constitution, which provides for the protection of the first and the assurance of the second by the establishment of a World Ombudsmus to carry out precisely the function that Amnesty is now assuming. The only difference is that under a World Executive with power to enforce its laws, the ombudsmen could legally compel a proper investigation and prosecution of the detected cases of infringement, and a federal World Administration could make its writ effective; whereas Amnesty is unable to compel even so much as an impartial enquiry into the cases that it reports. To achieve its aims, therefore, Amnesty International must join in the campaign to ratify the Constitution for the Federation of Earth and apply its skills and its energies as much to advertising that as to detecting violations of human rights.

THE REQUIRED PLAN OF ACTION

The majority of people all over the world are so engrossed in the demands made on them by their proximal needs and interests, many are so desperately preoccupied by the effort to provide themselves with the common necessities of life, that they are unaware or unheedful of the global perils in which they all stand. The better off are mostly too involved with the furtherance of their own selfish aims to take cognizance of them; the worse off are under too much pressure merely to survive to attend to them. Millions are not even aware of their existence and nature. Politicians are more concerned with their chances of re-election than with the necessity for world government, and what the electors do not emphatically demand, the politicians will not volunteer to provide.

At the moment public attention is engrossed by the horrors being perpetrated in Yugoslavia and the misery being endured by the people of Somalia, and little heed is being given to the larger problems that threaten to engulf the entire population of the Earth. These immediate and crying needs are little more than indicators of the wrath to come unless more radical and more wide-ranging measures are taken to save mankind from its present predicament.

In times of great stress, however, in times of war, or in the aftermath of some great natural disaster, people are apt to forget their conflicting personal objectives and to unite in their efforts to support and further the common welfare. Today the threat to human survival is worldwide and is vastly greater than that of any prospect of military invasion, or localized natural cataclysm. If only the mass of the people can be apprised of their common danger and be persuaded that the only chance to overcome it requires the establishment of world government, they should be intelligent enough to unite in their demand for it and to put pressure on their governments to ratify the Constitution for the Federation of Earth.

For this reason, all the non-governmental organizations mentioned above must now join forces with the numerous others of like kind, with World Federalists and with the WCPA in a vigorous campaign to put popular pressure on national governments to ratify and bring into force the World Constitution by every approved procedure. In a combined effort they must bang on the doors of the media and persuade them to publicize the draft constitution, to invite discussion of it, both criticism and defense, and to report on the campaign for its ratification. At the same time, fund-raising efforts for the campaign must be organized, and the WCPA should be enabled to emulate Greenpeace, by chartering one or more aircraft (rather than ships) in which it can send teams of lecturers around the world to alert people everywhere, more fully than is yet apparent, to the perils in which they stand, to explain why world federation is the only path to the removal of threats to survival and the only hope for the solution of world problems, to inform them about the constitution, and to advocate its adoption. Finally, they must exhort the people of the Earth to elect to their parliaments representatives who support world government and will induce their legislatures to ratify the World Constitution. And if, in the countries where they live, there are dictators in power, they must agitate for world government with such insistence that their rulers cannot safely resist the pressure to ratify the constitution. The campaign must become widely audible and visible; it must be persistent and unflagging; it must be unified, determined, and convincing.

Further, the ratification process once begun must be resolute and rapid, because the world cannot afford a protracted period of power politics, which will inevitably persist as long as states remain sovereign and independent; and a preliminary but incompletely comprehensive federation will have the status and remain in the situation of a contemporary sovereign state until it embraces the whole world. The ratification process must, therefore, proceed apace, to bring all nations under the jurisdiction of the World Constitution and the World Judiciary with the least possible delay. Meanwhile, in the preliminary stages, the provisional World Parliament must press ahead with the demarcation of administrative and electoral regions and the organization of elections, to give the federal governing institutions the means of operation at the soonest possible moment.

THE PRICE OF FAILURE

If the Constitution for the Federation of Earth is not ratified, if no world union comes into being, and if nations remain sovereign, no new world order capable of coping with current major world problems will arise. Even if regional federations are formed (the probability of which at present is not very high, and the prospects of agreement where the process has begun are not very bright), the essential relationship between sovereign powers will remain unchanged. In that case, power politics will continue and the threat of war will be ever present, with a nuclear holocaust always looming in the background. Even without the use of nuclear weapons modern warfare can be fatally devastating to the whole world community through its impact on the environment as well as its destructive potential to civilized order.

Further, the present international dispensation gives no promise of concerted action to counter the rapid deterioration of the environment now in progress. Population will multiply uncontrolled, urban sprawl will overrun arable land, domestic and industrial waste, much of it lethal, will accumulate. Forests will continue to disappear; deserts will expand; rivers, lakes, estuaries, and seas will become more and more polluted; wetlands will be lost; living species will become extinct; global warming will increase and climatic catastrophe approach at an accelerating pace; the protective ozone layer will dissipate and terrestrial life, vulnerable to ultraviolet radiation, will succumb; the food chain will disintegrate and the millions of people facing starvation will multiply. For how long the human race, or any life at all, can survive such mutually exacerbating and augmenting destructive influences is more than doubtful.

If all this is to be prevented, there is no viable alternative to world federation. Although in itself it is not the solution of the major problems, if any solution at all is to be possible and practicable, it is the indispensable prior condition; so a vigorous and determined global campaign must be conducted without delay, as we have described it above, for the ratification of the Constitution for the Federation of Earth—a concerted campaign, in which all the appropriate organizations and societies must join—to inform and educate the peoples of the world of the enormity of the dangers and of the indispensability of the required world order.

Unless this can be done, and unless the population of the world can be made to see why it must be done, no legal machinery will be available to ensure that the critical problems of global warming, climate change, the poisoning of the hydrosphere and the atmosphere, the control of nuclear radiation, and the maintenance of world peace can be addressed with any prospect of success. The water in which the frog had been lulled to sleep will boil and the poor creature will succumb in consequence of its own inactivity. Mankind will indeed face extinction, along with other living creatures. The fruits of culture will be lost forever; the light of knowledge will be extinguished, and the discoveries of science will have been in vain; the illumination of self-consciousness will vanish from the Earth, abandoning it to oblivion as it becomes a dead planet, like Mars or Venus.

Federalists of the Earth unite; we have everything to lose if you fail!

Appendix

A
Constitution
for the Federation
of Earth

Contents

PREAMBLE

Realizing that Humanity today has come to a turning point in history and that we are on the threshold of a new world order which promises to usher in an era of peace, prosperity, justice and harmony;

Aware of the interdependence of people, nations and all life;

Aware that man's abuse of science and technology has brought Humanity to the brink of disaster through the production of horrendous weaponry of mass destruction and to the brink of ecological and social catastrophe;

Aware that the traditional concept of security through military defense is a total illusion both for the present and for the future;

Aware of the misery and conflicts caused by ever increasing disparity between rich and poor;

Conscious of our obligation to posterity to save Humanity from imminent and total annihilation;

Conscious that Humanity is One despite the existence of diverse nations, races, creeds, ideologies and cultures and that the principle of unity in diversity is the basis for a new age when war shall be outlawed and peace prevail; when the earth's total resources shall be equitably used for human welfare; and when basic human rights and responsibilities shall be shared by all without discrimination;

Conscious of the inescapable reality that the greatest hope for the survival of life on earth is the establishment of a democratic world government;

We, citizens of the world, hereby resolve to establish a world federation to be governed in accordance with this constitution for the Federation of Earth.

A CONSTITUTION FOR THE FEDERATION OF EARTH

ARTICLE I
BROAD FUNCTIONS OF THE FEDERATION OF EARTH

The broad functions of the Federation of Earth shall be:

1. To prevent war, secure disarmament, and resolve territorial and other disputes which endanger peace and human rights.

2. To protect universal human rights, including life, liberty, security, democracy, and equal opportunities in life.

3. To obtain for all people on earth the conditions required for equitable economic and social development and for diminishing social differences.

4. To regulate world trade, communications, transportation, currency, standards, use of world resources, and other global and international processes.

5. To protect the environment and the ecological fabric of life from all sources of damage, and to control technological innovations whose effects transcend national boundaries, for the purpose of keeping Earth a safe, healthy and happy home for humanity.

6. To devise and implement solutions to all problems which are beyond the capacity of national governments, or which are now or may become of global or international concern or consequence.

ARTICLE II
BASIC STRUCTURE OF THE WORLD FEDERATION AND WORLD GOVERNMENT

1. The Federation of Earth shall be organized as a universal federation, to include all nations and all people, and to encompass all oceans, seas and lands of Earth, inclusive of non-self governing territories, together with the surrounding atmosphere.

2. The World Government for the Federation of Earth shall be non-military and shall be democratic in its own structure, with ultimate sovereignty residing in all the people who live on Earth.

3. The authority and powers granted to the World Government shall be limited to those defined in this Constitution for the Federation of Earth, applicable to problems and affairs which transcend national

boundaries, leaving to national governments jurisdiction over the internal affairs of the respective nations but consistent with the authority of the World Government to protect universal human rights as defined in this World Constitution.

4. The basic direct electoral and administrative units of the World Government shall be World Electoral and Administrative Districts. A total of not more than 1000 World Electoral and Administrative Districts shall be defined, and shall be nearly equal in population, within the limits of plus or minus ten percent.

5. Contiguous World Electoral and Administrative Districts shall be combined as may be appropriate to compose a total of twenty World Electoral and Administrative Regions for the following purposes, but not limited thereto; for the election or appointment of certain world government officials; for administrative purposes; for composing various organs of the world government as enumerated in Article IV; for the functioning of the Judiciary, the Enforcement System, and the Ombudsmus, as well as for the functioning of any other organ or agency of the World Government.

6. The World Electoral and Administrative Regions may be composed of a variable number of World Electoral and Administrative Districts, taking into consideration geographic, cultural, ecological and other factors as well as population.

7. Contiguous World Electoral and Administrative Regions shall be grouped together in pairs to compose Magna-Regions.

8. The boundaries for World Electoral and Administrative Regions shall not cross the boundaries of the World Electoral and Administrative Districts, and shall be common insofar as feasible for the various administrative departments and for the several organs and agencies of the World Government. Boundaries for the World Electoral and Administrative Districts as well as for the Regions need not conform to existing national boundaries, but shall conform as far as practicable.

9. The World Electoral and Administrative Regions shall be grouped to compose at least five Continental Divisions of the Earth, for the election or appointment of certain world government officials, and for certain aspects of the composition and functioning of the several organs and agencies of the World Government as specified hereinafter. The boundaries of Continental Divisions shall not cross existing national boundaries as far as practicable. Continental Divisions may be composed of a variable number of World Electoral and Administrative Regions.

ARTICLE III
ORGANS OF THE WORLD GOVERNMENT

The organs of the World Government shall be:
1. The World Parliament
2. The World Executive
3. The World Administration
4. The Integrative Complex
5. The World Judiciary
6. The Enforcement System
7. The World Ombudsmus

ARTICLE IV
GRANT OF SPECIFIC POWERS TO THE WORLD GOVERNMENT

The powers of the World Government to be exercised through its several organs and agencies shall comprise the following:

1. Prevent wars and armed conflicts among the nations, regions, districts, parts and peoples of the Earth.
2. Supervise disarmament and prevent re-armament; prohibit and eliminate the design, testing, manufacture, sale, purchase, use and possession of weapons of mass destruction, and prohibit or regulate all lethal weapons which the World Parliament may decide.
3. Prohibit incitement to war, and discrimination against or defamation of conscientious objectors.
4. Provide the means for peaceful and just resolution of disputes and conflicts among or between nations, peoples, and/or other components within the Federation of Earth.
5. Supervise boundary settlements and conduct plebiscites as needed.
6. Define the boundaries for the districts, regions and divisions which are established for electoral, administrative, judicial and other purposes of the World Government.
7. Define and regulate procedures for the nomination and election of the members of each House of the World Parliament, and for the nomination, election, appointment and employment of all World Government officials and personnel.
8. Codify world laws, including the body of international law developed prior to adoption of the world constitution, but not inconsistent therewith, and which is approved by the World Parliament.

9. Establish universal standards for weights, measurements, accounting and records.

10. Provide assistance in the event of large scale calamities, including drought, famine, pestilence, flood, earthquake, hurricane, ecological disruptions and other disasters.

11. Guarantee and enforce the civil liberties and the basic human rights which are defined in the Bill of Rights for the Citizens of Earth which is made a part of this World Constitution under Article XII.

12. Define standards and promote the worldwide improvement in working conditions, nutrition, health, housing, human settlements, environmental conditions, education, economic security, and other conditions defined under Article XII of this World Constitution.

13. Regulate and supervise international transportation, communications, postal services, and migrations of people.

14. Regulate and supervise supra-national trade, industry, corporations, businesses, cartels, professional services, labor supply, finances, investments and insurance.

15. Secure and supervise the elimination of tariffs and other trade barriers among nations, but with provisions to prevent or minimize hardship for those previously protected by tariffs.

16. Raise the revenues and funds, by direct and/or indirect means, which are necessary for the purposes and activities of the World Government.

17. Establish and operate world financial, banking, credit and insurance institutions designed to serve human needs; establish, issue and regulate world currency, credit and exchange.

18. Plan for and regulate the development, use, conservation and recycling of the natural resources of Earth as the common heritage of Humanity; protect the environment in every way for the benefit of both present and future generations.

19. Create and operate a World Economic Development Organization to serve equitably the needs of all nations and people included within the World Federation.

20. Develop and implement solutions to transnational problems of food supply, agricultural production, soil fertility, soil conservation, pest control, diet, nutrition, drugs and poisons; control the disposal of toxic wastes.

21. Develop and implement means to control population growth in relation to the life-support capacities of Earth, and solve problems of population distribution.

22. Develop, protect, regulate and conserve the water supplies of Earth;

develop, operate and/or coordinate transnational irrigation and other water supply and control projects; assure equitable allocation of transnational water supplies, and protect against adverse transnational effects of water or moisture diversion or weather control projects within national boundaries.

23. Own, administer and supervise the development and conservation of the oceans and sea-beds of Earth and all resources thereof, and protect from damage.

24. Protect from damage, and control and supervise the uses of the atmosphere of Earth.

25. Conduct inter-planetary and cosmic explorations and research; have exclusive jurisdiction over the Moon and over all satellites launched from Earth.

26. Establish, operate and/or coordinate global air lines, ocean transport systems, international railways and highways, global communication systems, and means for interplanetary travel and communications; control and administer vital waterways.

27. Develop, operate and/or coordinate transnational power systems, or networks of small units, integrating into the systems or networks power derived from the sun, wind, water, tides, heat differentials, magnetic forces, and any other source of safe, ecologically sound and continuing energy supply.

28. Control the mining, production, transportation and use of fossil sources of energy to the extent necessary to reduce and prevent damages to the environment and the ecology, as well as to prevent conflicts and conserve supplies for sustained use by succeeding generations.

29. Exercise exclusive jurisdiction and control over nuclear energy research and testing and nuclear power production, including the right to prohibit any form of testing or production considered hazardous.

30. Place under world controls essential natural resources which may be limited or unevenly distributed about the Earth. Find and implement ways to reduce wastes and find ways to minimize disparities when development or production is insufficient to supply everybody with all that may be needed.

31. Provide for the examination and assessment of technological innovations which are or may be of supranational consequence, to determine possible hazards or perils to humanity or the environment; institute such controls and regulations of technology as may be found necessary to prevent or correct widespread hazards or perils to human health and welfare.

32. Carry out intensive programs to develop safe alternatives to any technology or technological processes which may be hazardous to the environment, the ecological system, or human health and welfare.

33. Resolve supra-national problems caused by gross disparities in technological development or capability, capital formation, availability of natural resources, educational opportunity, economic opportunity, and wage and price differentials. Assist the processes of technology transfer under conditions which safeguard human welfare and the environment and contribute to minimizing disparities.

34. Intervene under procedures to be defined by the World Parliament in cases of either intra-state violence or intra-state problems which seriously affect world peace or universal human rights.

35. Develop a world university system. Obtain the correction of prejudicial communicative materials which cause misunderstandings or conflicts due to differences of race, religion, sex, national origin or affiliation.

36. Organize, coordinate and/or administer a voluntary, non-military World Service Corps, to carry out a wide variety of projects designed to serve human welfare.

37. Designate as may be found desirable an official world language or official world languages.

38. Establish and operate a system of world parks, wild life preserves, natural places, and wilderness areas.

39. Define and establish procedures for initiative and referendum by the Citizens of Earth on matters of supranational legislation not prohibited by this World Constitution.

40. Establish such departments, bureaus, commissions, institutes, corporations, administrations, or agencies as may be needed to carry out any and all of the functions and powers of the World Government.

41. Serve the needs of humanity in any and all ways which are now, or may prove in the future to be, beyond the capacity of national and local governments.

ARTICLE V
THE WORLD PARLIAMENT

SECTION A.   FUNCTIONS AND POWERS OF
THE WORLD PARLIAMENT

The functions and powers of the World Parliament shall comprise the following:

1. To prepare and enact detailed legislation in all areas of authority and jurisdiction granted to the World Government under Article IV of this World Constitution.

2. To amend or repeal world laws as may be found necessary or desirable.

3. To approve, amend or reject the international laws developed prior to the advent of World Government, and to codify and integrate the system of world law and world legislation under the World Government.

4. To establish such regulations and directions as may be needed, consistent with this world constitution, for the proper functioning of all organs, branches, departments, bureaus, commissions, institutes, agencies or parts of the World Government.

5. To review, amend and give final approval to each budget for the World Government, as submitted by the World Executive; to devise the specific means for directly raising the funds needed to fulfill the budget, including taxes, licenses, fees, globally accounted social and public costs which must be added into the prices for goods and services, loans and credit advances, and any other appropriate means; and to appropriate and allocate funds for all operations and functions of the World Government in accordance with approved budgets, but subject to the right of the Parliament to revise any appropriation not yet spent or contractually committed.

6. To create, alter, abolish or consolidate the departments, bureaus, commissions, institutes, agencies or other parts of the World Government as may be needed for the best functioning of the several organs of the World Government, subject to the specific provisions of this World Constitution.

7. To approve the appointments of the heads of all major departments, commissions, offices, agencies and other parts of the several organs of the World Government, except those chosen by electoral or civil service procedures.

8. To remove from office for cause any member of the World Executive, and any elective or appointive head of any organ, department, office, agency or other part of the World Government, subject to the

specific provisions in this World Constitution concerning specific offices.

9. To define and revise the boundaries of the World Electoral and Administrative Districts, the World Electoral and Administrative Regions and Magna Regions, and the Continental Divisions.

10. To schedule the implementation of those provisions of the World Constitution which require implementation by stages during the several stages of Provisional World Government, First Operative Stage of World Government, Second Operative Stage of World Government, and Full Operative Stage of World Government, as defined in Articles XVII and XIX of this World Constitution.

11. To plan and schedule the implementation of those provisions of the World Constitution which may require a period of years to be accomplished.

SECTION B.   COMPOSITION OF THE WORLD PARLIAMENT

1. The World Parliament shall be composed of three houses, designated as follows:
The House of Peoples, to represent the people of Earth directly and equally;
The House of Nations, to represent the nations which are joined together in the Federation of Earth; and a House of Counsellors with particular functions to represent the highest good and best interests of humanity as a whole.

2. All members of the World Parliament, regardless of House, shall be designated as Members of the World Parliament.

SECTION C.   THE HOUSE OF PEOPLES

1. The House of Peoples shall be composed of the people's delegates directly elected in proportion to population from the World Electoral and Administrative Districts, as defined in Article II-4.

2. People's delegates shall be elected by universal adult suffrage, open to all persons of age 18 and above.

3. One people's delegate shall be elected from each World Electoral and Administrative District to serve a five year term in the House of Peoples. People's delegates may be elected to serve successive terms without limit. Each people's delegate shall have one vote.

4. A candidate for election to serve as a people's delegate must be at least 21 years of age, a resident for at least one year of the electoral district from which the candidate is seeking election, and shall take a pledge of service to humanity.

SECTION D.   THE HOUSE OF NATIONS

1. The House of Nations shall be composed of National Delegates
   elected or appointed by procedures to be determined by each national
   government on the following basis:
   a) One national delegate from each nation of at least 100,000 popula-
      tion, but less than 10,000,000 population.
   b) Two national delegates from each nation of at least 10,000,000
      population, but less than 100,000,000 population.
   c) Three national delegates from each nation of 100,000,000 popula-
      tion or more.

2. Nations of less than 100,000 population may join in groups with other
   nations for purposes of representation in the House of Nations.

3. National delegates shall be elected or appointed to serve for terms of
   five years, and may be elected or appointed to serve successive terms
   without limit. Each national delegate shall have one vote.

4. Any person to serve as a national delegate shall be a citizen for at least
   two years of the nation to be represented, must be at least 21 years of
   age, and shall take a pledge of service to humanity.

SECTION E.   THE HOUSE OF COUNSELLORS

1. The House of Counsellors shall be composed of 200 counsellors
   chosen in equal numbers from nominations submitted from the twenty World Electoral and Administrative Regions, as defined in Article
   II–5 and II–6, i.e., ten from each Region.

2. Nominations for members of the House of Counsellors shall be made
   by the teachers and students at the universities and colleges and of
   scientific academies and institutes within each world electoral and
   administrative region. Nominees may be persons who are off campus
   in any walk of life as well as on campus.

3. Nominees to the House of Counsellors from each World Electoral and
   Administrative Region shall, by vote taken among themselves, reduce
   the number of nominees to no less than two times and no more than
   three times the number to be elected.

4. Nominees to serve as members of the House of Counsellors must be at
   least 25 years of age, and shall take a pledge of service to humanity.
   There shall be no residence requirement, and a nominee need not be a
   resident of the region from which nominated or elected.

5. The members of the House of Counsellors from each region shall be
   elected by the members of the other two houses of the World Parliament from the particular region.

6. Counsellors shall be elected to serve terms of ten years. One-half of the members of the House of Counsellors shall be elected every five years. Counsellors may serve successive terms without limit. Each Counsellor shall have one vote.

SECTION F.   PROCEDURES OF THE WORLD PARLIAMENT

1. Each house of the World Parliament during its first session after general elections shall elect a panel of five chairpersons from among its own members, one from each of five Continental Divisions. The chairpersons shall rotate annually so that each will serve for one year as chief presiding officer, while the other four serve as vice-chairpersons.

2. The panels of Chairpersons from each House shall meet together, as needed, for the purpose of coordinating the work of the Houses of the Parliament, both severally and jointly.

3. Any legislative measure or action may be initiated in either the House of Peoples or House of Nations or both concurrently, and shall become effective when passed by simple majority vote of both the House of Peoples and of the House of Nations, except in those cases where an absolute majority vote or other voting majority is specified in this World Constitution.

4. In case of deadlock on a measure initiated in either House of Peoples or House of Nations, the measure shall then automatically go to the House of Counsellors for decision by simple majority vote of the House of Counsellors, except in cases where other majority vote is required in this World Constitution. Any measure may be referred for decision to the House of Counsellors by a concurrent vote of the other two houses.

5. The House of Counsellors may initiate any legislative measure, which shall then be submitted to the other two houses and must be passed by simple majority vote of both the House of Peoples and House of Nations to become effective, unless other voting majority is required by some provision of this World Constitution.

6. The House of Counsellors may introduce an opinion or resolution on any measure pending before either of the other two houses; either of the other houses may request the opinion of the House of Counsellors before acting upon a measure.

7. Each house of the World Parliament shall adopt its own detailed rules of procedure, which shall be consistent with the procedures set forth in this World Constitution, and which shall be designed to facilitate coordinated functioning of the three houses.

8. Approval of appointments by the World Parliament or any house thereof shall require simple majority votes, while removals for cause shall require absolute majority votes.

9. After the full operative stage of World Government is declared, general elections for members of the World Parliament to the House of Peoples shall be held every five years. The first general elections shall be held within the first two years following the declaration of the full operative stage of World Government.

10. Until the full operative stage of World Government is declared, elections for members of the World Parliament to the House of Peoples may be conducted whenever feasible in relation to the campaign for ratification of this World Constitution.

11. Regular sessions of the House of Peoples and House of Nations of the World Parliament shall convene on the second Monday of January of each and every Year.

12. Each nation, according to its own procedures, shall appoint or elect members of the World Parliament to the House of Nations at least thirty days prior to the date for convening the World Parliament in January.

13. The House of Peoples together with the House of Nations shall elect the members of the World Parliament to the House of Counsellors during the month of January after the general elections. For its first session after general elections, the House of Counsellors shall convene on the second Monday of March, and thereafter concurrently with the other two houses.

14. Bi-elections to fill vacancies shall be held within three months from occurrence of the vacancy or vacancies.

15. The World Parliament shall remain in session for a minimum of nine months of each year. One or two breaks may be taken during each year, at times and for durations to be decided by simple majority vote of the House of Peoples and House of Nations sitting jointly.

16. Annual salaries for members of the World Parliament of all three houses shall be the same, except for those who serve also as members of the Presidium and of the Executive Cabinet.

17. Salary schedules for members of the World Parliament and for members of the Presidium and of the Executive Cabinet shall be determined by the World Parliament.

ARTICLE VI
THE WORLD EXECUTIVE

SECTION A.   FUNCTIONS AND POWERS OF THE WORLD EXECUTIVE

1. To implement the basic system of world law as defined in the World Constitution and in the codified system of world law after approval by the World Parliament.

2. To implement legislation enacted by the World Parliament.

3. To propose and recommend legislation for enactment by the World Parliament.

4. To convene the World Parliament in special sessions when necessary.

5. To supervise the World Administration and the Integrative Complex and all of the departments, bureaus, offices, institutes and agencies thereof.

6. To nominate, select and remove the heads of various organs, branches, departments, bureaus, offices, commissions, institutes, agencies and other parts of the World Government, in accordance with the provisions of this World Constitution and as specified in measures enacted by the World Parliament.

7. To prepare and submit annually to the World Parliament a comprehensive budget for the operations of the World Government, and to prepare and submit periodically budget projections over periods of several years.

8. To define and propose priorities for world legislation and budgetary allocations.

9. To be held accountable to the World Parliament for the expenditures of appropriations made by the World Parliament in accordance with approved and longer term budgets, subject to revisions approved by the World Parliament.

SECTION B.   COMPOSITION OF THE WORLD EXECUTIVE

The World Executive shall consist of a Presidium of five members, and of an Executive Cabinet of from twenty to thirty members, all of whom shall be members of the World Parliament.

SECTION C.   THE PRESIDIUM

1. The Presidium shall be composed of five members, one to be designated as President and the other four to be designated as Vice Presidents. Each member of the Presidium shall be from a different Continental Division.

2. The Presidency of the Presidium shall rotate each year, with each member in turn to serve as President, while the other four serve as Vice Presidents. The order of rotation shall be decided by the Presidium.

3. The decisions of the Presidium shall be taken collectively, on the basis of majority decisions.

4. Each member of the Presidium shall be a member of the World Parliament, either elected to the House of Peoples or to the House of Counsellors, or appointed or elected to the House of Nations.

5. Nominations for the Presidium shall be made by the House of Counsellors. The number of nominees shall be from two to three times the number to be elected. No more than one-third of the nominees shall be from the House of Counsellors or from the House of Nations, and nominees must be included from all Continental Divisions.

6. From among the nominees submitted by the House of Counsellors, the Presidium shall be elected by vote of the combined membership of all three houses of the World Parliament in joint session. A plurality vote equal to at least 40 percent of the total membership of the World Parliament shall be required for the election of each member to the Presidium, with successive elimination votes taken as necessary until the required plurality is achieved.

7. Members of the Presidium may be removed for cause, either individually or collectively, by an absolute majority vote of the combined membership of the three houses of the World Parliament in joint session.

8. The term of office for the Presidium shall be five years and shall run concurrently with the terms of office for the members as Members of the World Parliament, except that at the end of each five year period, the Presidium members in office shall continue to serve until the new Presidium for the succeeding term is elected. Membership in the Presidium shall be limited to two consecutive terms.

SECTION D.   THE EXECUTIVE CABINET

1. The Executive Cabinet shall be composed of from twenty to thirty members, with at least one member from each of the ten World Electoral and Administrative Magna Regions of the world.

2. All members of the Executive Cabinet shall be Members of the World Parliament.

3. There shall be no more than two members of the Executive Cabinet from any single nation of the World Federation. There may be only one member of the Executive Cabinet from a nation from which a

Member of the World Parliament is serving as a member of the Presidium.

4. Each member of the Executive Cabinet shall serve as the head of a department or agency of the World Administration or Integrative Complex, and in this capacity shall be designated as Minister of the particular department or agency.

5. Nominations for members of the Executive Cabinet shall be made by the Presidium, taking into consideration the various functions which Executive Cabinet members are to perform. The Presidium shall nominate no more than two times the number to be elected.

6. The Executive Cabinet shall be elected by simple majority vote of the combined membership of all three houses of the World Parliament in joint session.

7. Members of the Executive Cabinet either individually or collectively may be removed for cause by an absolute majority vote of the combined membership of all three houses of the World Parliament sitting in joint session.

8. The term of office in the Executive Cabinet shall be five years, and shall run concurrently with the terms of office for the members as Members of the World Parliament, except that at the end of each five year period, the Cabinet members in office shall continue to serve until the new Executive Cabinet for the succeeding term is elected. Membership in the Executive Cabinet shall be limited to three consecutive terms, regardless of change in ministerial position.

SECTION E.   PROCEDURES OF THE WORLD EXECUTIVE

1. The Presidium shall assign the ministerial positions among the Cabinet members to head the several administrative departments and major agencies of the Administration and of the Integrative Complex. Each Vice President may also serve as a Minister to head an administrative department, but not the President. Ministerial positions may be changed at the discretion of the Presidium. A Cabinet member or Vice President may hold more than one ministerial post, but no more than three, providing that no Cabinet member is without a Ministerial post.

2. The Presidium, in consultation with the Executive Cabinet, shall prepare and present to the World Parliament near the beginning of each year a proposed program of world legislation. The Presidium may propose other legislation during the year.

3. The Presidium, in consultation with the Executive Cabinet, and in consultation with the World Financial Administration, (see Article VIII, Sec. G-1-h) shall be responsible for preparing and submitting to

the World Parliament the proposed annual budget, and budgetary projections over periods of years.

4. Each Cabinet Member and Vice President as Minister of a particular department or agency shall prepare an annual report for the particular department or agency, to be submitted both to the Presidium and to the World Parliament.

5. The members of the Presidium and of the Executive Cabinet at all times shall be responsible both individually and collectively to the World Parliament.

6. Vacancies occurring at any time in the World Executive shall be filled within sixty days by nomination and election in the same manner as specified for filling the offices originally.

SECTION F. LIMITATIONS ON THE WORLD EXECUTIVE

1. The World Executive shall not at any time alter, suspend, abridge, infringe or otherwise violate any provision of this World Constitution or any legislation or world law enacted or approved by the World Parliament in accordance with the provisions of this World Constitution.

2. The World Executive shall not have veto power over any legislation passed by the World Parliament.

3. The World Executive may not dissolve the World Parliament or any House of the World Parliament.

4. The World Executive may not act contrary to decisions of the World Courts.

5. The World Executive shall be bound to faithfully execute all legislation passed by the World Parliament in accordance with the provisions of this World Constitution, and may not impound or refuse to spend funds appropriated by the World Parliament, nor spend more funds than are appropriated by the World Parliament.

6. The World Executive may not transcend or contradict the decisions or controls of the World Parliament, the World Judiciary or the Provisions of this World Constitution by any device of executive order or executive privilege or emergency declaration or decree.

ARTICLE VII
THE WORLD ADMINISTRATION

SECTION A. FUNCTIONS OF THE WORLD ADMINISTRATION

1. The World Administration shall be organized to carry out the detailed

and continuous administration and implementation of world legislation and world law.

2. The World Administration shall be under the direction of the World Executive, and shall at all times be responsible to the World Executive.

3. The World Administration shall be organized so as to give professional continuity to the work of administration and implementation.

SECTION B.   STRUCTURE AND PROCEDURE OF THE WORLD ADMINISTRATION

1. The World Administration shall be composed of professionally organized departments and other agencies in all areas of activity requiring continuity of administration and implementation by the World Government.

2. Each Department or major agency of the World Administration shall be headed by a Minister who shall be either a member of the Executive Cabinet or a Vice President of the Presidium.

3. Each Department or major agency of the World Administration shall have as chief of staff a Senior Administrator, who shall assist the Minister and supervise the detailed work of the Department or agency.

4. Each Senior Administrator shall be nominated by the Minister of the particular Department or agency from among persons in the senior lists of the World Civil Service Administration, as soon as senior lists have been established by the World Civil Service Administration, and shall be confirmed by the Presidium. Temporary qualified appointments shall be made by the Ministers, with confirmation by the Presidium, pending establishment of the senior lists.

5. There shall be a Secretary General of the World Administration, who shall be nominated by the Presidium and confirmed by absolute majority vote of the entire Executive Cabinet.

6. The functions and responsibilities of the Secretary General of the World Administration shall be to assist in coordinating the work of the Senior Administrators of the several Departments and agencies of the World Administration. The Secretary General shall at all times be subject to the direction of the Presidium, and shall be directly responsible to the Presidium.

7. The employment of any Senior Administrator and of the Secretary General may be terminated for cause by absolute majority vote of both the Executive Cabinet and Presidium combined, but not contrary to civil service rules which protect tenure on grounds of competence.

8. Each Minister of a Department or agency of the World Administration, being also a Member of the World Parliament, shall provide continuous liaison between the particular Department or agency and the World Parliament, shall respond at any time to any questions or requests for information from the Parliament, including committees of any House of the World Parliament.

9. The Presidium, in cooperation with the particular Ministers in each case, shall be responsible for the original organization of each of the Departments and major agencies of the World Administration.

10. The assignment of legislative measures, constitutional provisions and areas of world law to particular Departments and agencies for administration and implementation shall be done by the Presidium in consultation with the Executive Cabinet and Secretary General, unless specifically provided in legislation passed by the World Parliament.

11. The Presidium, in consultation with the Executive Cabinet, may propose the creation of other departments and agencies to have ministerial status; and may propose the alteration, combination or termination of existing Departments and agencies of ministerial status as may seem necessary or desirable. Any such creation, alteration, combination or termination shall require a simple majority vote of approval of the three houses of the World Parliament in joint session.

12. The World Parliament by absolute majority vote of the three houses in joint session may specify the creation of new departments or agencies of ministerial status in the World Administration, or may direct the World Executive to alter, combine, or terminate existing departments or agencies of ministerial status.

13. The Presidium and the World Executive may not create, establish or maintain any administrative or executive department or agency for the purpose of circumventing control by the World Parliament.

SECTION C.   DEPARTMENTS OF THE WORLD ADMINISTRATION

Among the Departments and agencies of the World Administration of ministerial status, but not limited thereto and subject to combinations and to changes in descriptive terminology, shall be those listed under this Section. Each major area of administration shall be headed by a Cabinet Minister and a Senior Administrator, or by a Vice President and a Senior Administrator.

1. Disarmament and War Prevention

2. Population

3. Food and Agriculture

4. Water Supplies and Waterways

5. Health and Nutrition

6. Education

7. Cultural Diversity and the Arts

8. Habitat and Settlement
9. Environment and Ecology
10. World Resources
11. Oceans and Seabeds
12. Atmosphere and Space
13. Energy
14. Science and Technology
15. Genetic Research and Engineering
16. Labor and Income
17. Economic and Social Development
18. Commerce and Industry
19. Transportation and Travel
20. Multi-National Corporations
21. Communications and Information
22. Human Rights
23. Distributive Justice
24. World Service Corps
25. World Territories, Capitals and Parks
26. Exterior Relations
27. Democratic Procedures
28. Revenue

ARTICLE VIII
THE INTEGRATIVE COMPLEX

SECTION A.   DEFINITION

1. Certain administrative, research, planning and facilitative agencies of the World Government which are particularly essential for the satisfactory functioning of all or most aspects of the World Government shall be designated as the Integrative Complex. The Integrative Complex shall include the agencies listed under this Section, with the proviso that other such agencies may be added upon recommendation of the Presidium followed by decision of the World Parliament.

   a) The World Civil Service Administration
   b) The World Boundaries and Elections Administration
   c) The Institute on Governmental Procedures and World Problems
   d) The Agency for Research and Planning
   e) The Agency for Technological and Environmental Assessment
   f) The World Financial Administration

2. Each agency of the Integrative Complex shall be headed by a Cabinet Minister and a Senior Administrator, or by a Vice President and a Senior Administrator, together with a Commission as provided hereunder. The rules of procedure for each agency shall be decided by majority decision of the Commission members together with the Administrator and the Minister or Vice President.

3. The World Parliament may at any time define further the responsibili-

ties, functioning and organization of the several agencies of the Integrative Complex, consistent with the provisions of Article VIII and other provisions of the World Constitution.

4. Each agency of the Integrative Complex shall make an annual report to the World Parliament and to the Presidium.

SECTION B.   THE WORLD CIVIL SERVICE ADMINISTRATION

1. The functions of the World Civil Service Administration shall be the following, but not limited thereto:

   a) To formulate and define standards, qualifications, tests, examinations and salary scales for the personnel of all organs, departments, bureaus, offices, commissions and agencies of the World Government, in conformity with the provisions of this World Constitution and requiring approval by the Presidium and Executive Cabinet, subject to review and approval by the World Parliament.

   b) To establish rosters or lists of competent personnel for all categories of personnel to be appointed or employed in the service of the World Government.

   c) To select and employ upon request by any government organ, department, bureau, office, institute, commission, agency or authorized official, such competent personnel as may be needed and authorized, except for those positions which are made elective or appointive under provisions of the World Constitution or by specific legislation of the World Parliament.

2. The World Civil Service Administration shall be headed by a ten member commission in addition to the Cabinet Minister or Vice President and Senior Administrator. The Commission shall be composed of one commissioner from each of ten World Electoral and Administrative Magna-Regions. The persons to serve as Commissioners shall be nominated by the House of Counsellors and then appointed by the Presidium for five year terms. Commissioners may serve consecutive terms.

SECTION C.   THE WORLD BOUNDARIES AND ELECTIONS ADMINISTRATION

1. The functions of the World Boundaries and Elections Administration shall include the following, but not limited thereto:

   a) To define the boundaries for the basic World Electoral and Administrative Districts, the World Electoral and Administrative Regions and Magna-Regions, and the Continental Divisions, for submission to the World Parliament for approval by legislative action.

b) To make periodic adjustments every ten or five years, as needed, of the boundaries for the World Electoral and Administrative Districts, the World Electoral and Administrative Regions and Magna-Regions, and of the Continental Divisions, subject to approval by the World Parliament.

c) To define the detailed procedures for the nomination and election of Members of the World Parliament to the House of Peoples and to the House of Counsellors, subject to approval by the World Parliament.

d) To conduct the elections for Members of the World Parliament to the House of Peoples and to the House of Counsellors.

e) Before each World Parliamentary Election, to prepare Voters' Information Booklets which shall summarize major current public issues, and shall list each candidate for elective office together with standard information about each candidate, and give space for each candidate to state his or her views on the defined major issues as well as on any other major issue of choice; to include information on any initiatives or referendums which are to be voted upon; to distribute the Voters' Information Booklets for each World Electoral District, or suitable group of Districts; and to obtain the advice of the Institute on Governmental Procedures and World Problems, the Agency for Research and Planning, and the Agency for Technological and Environmental Assessment in preparing the booklets.

f) To define the rules for world political parties, subject to approval by the World Parliament, and subject to review and recommendations of the World Ombudsmus.

g) To define the detailed procedures for legislative initiative and referendum by the Citizens of Earth, and to conduct voting on supra-national or global initiatives and referendums in conjunction with world parliamentary elections.

h) To conduct plebiscites when requested by other Organs of the World Government, and to make recommendations for the settlement of boundary disputes.

i) To conduct a global census every five years, and to prepare and maintain complete demographic analyses for Earth.

2. The World Boundaries and Elections Administration shall be headed by a ten member commission in addition to the Senior Administrator and the Cabinet Minister or Vice President. The commission shall be composed of one commissioner each from ten World Electoral and Administrative Magna-Regions. The persons to serve as commis-

sioners shall be nominated by the House of Counsellors and then appointed by the World Presidium for five year terms. Commissioners may serve consecutive terms.

SECTION D.   THE INSTITUTE ON GOVERNMENTAL PROCEDURES AND WORLD PROBLEMS

1. The functions of the Institute on Governmental Procedures and World Problems shall be as follows, but not limited thereto:

   a) To prepare and conduct courses of information, education and training for all personnel in the service of the World Government, including Members of the World Parliament and of all other elective, appointive and civil service personnel, so that every person in the service of the World Government may have a better understanding of the functions, structure, procedures and interrelationships of the various organs, departments, bureaus, offices, institutes, commissions, agencies and other parts of the World Government.

   b) To prepare and conduct courses and seminars for information, education, discussion, updating and new ideas in all areas of world problems, particularly for Members of the World Parliament and of the World Executive, and for the chief personnel of all organs, departments and agencies of the World Government, but open to all in the service of the World Government.

   c) To bring in qualified persons from private and public universities, colleges and research and action organizations of many countries, as well as other qualified persons, to lecture and to be resource persons for the courses and seminars organized by the Institute on Governmental Procedures and World Problems.

   d) To contract with private or public universities and colleges or other agencies to conduct courses and seminars for the Institute.

2. The Institute on Governmental Procedures and World Problems shall be supervised by a ten member commission in addition to the Senior Administrator and Cabinet Minister or Vice President. The commission shall be composed of one commissioner each to be named by the House of Peoples, the House of Nations, the House of Counsellors, the Presidium, the Collegium of World Judges, The World Ombudsmus, The World Attorneys General Office, the Agency for Research and Planning, the Agency for Technological and Environmental Assessment, and the World Financial Administration. Commissioners shall serve five year terms, and may serve consecutive terms.

SECTION E.   THE AGENCY FOR RESEARCH AND PLANNING

1. The functions of the Agency for Research and Planning shall be as follows, but not limited thereto:

   a) To serve the World Parliament, the World Executive, the World Administration, and other organs, departments and agencies of the World Government in any matter requiring research and planning within the competence of the agency.

   b) To prepare and maintain a comprehensive inventory of world resources.

   c) To prepare comprehensive long-range plans for the development, conservation, re-cycling and equitable sharing of the resources of Earth for the benefit of all people on Earth, subject to legislative action by the World Parliament.

   d) To prepare and maintain a comprehensive list and description of all world problems, including their inter-relationships, impact time projections and proposed solutions, together with bibliographies.

   e) To do research and help prepare legislative measures at the request of any Member of the World Parliament or of any committee of any House of the World Parliament.

   f) To do research and help prepare proposed legislation or proposed legislative programs and schedules at the request of the Presidium or Executive Cabinet or of any Cabinet Minister.

   g) To do research and prepare reports at the request of any other organ, department or agency of the World Government.

   h) To enlist the help of public and private universities, colleges, research agencies, and other associations and organizations for various research and planning projects.

   i) To contract with public and private universities, colleges, research agencies and other organizations for the preparation of specific reports, studies and proposals.

   j) To maintain a comprehensive World Library for the use of all Members of the World Parliament, and for the use of all other officials and persons in the service of the World Government, as well as for public information.

2. The Agency for Research and Planning shall be supervised by a ten member commission in addition to the Senior Administrator and Cabinet Minister or Vice President. The commission shall be composed of one commissioner each to be named by the House of Peoples, the House of Nations, the House of Counsellors, the Presidium, the Collegium of World Judges, the Office of World Attorneys General,

World Ombudsmus, the Agency for Technological and Environmental Assessment, the Institute on Governmental Procedures and World Problems, and the World Financial Administration. Commissioners shall serve five year terms, and may serve consecutive terms.

SECTION F.   THE AGENCY FOR TECHNOLOGICAL AND ENVIRONMENTAL ASSESSMENT

1. The functions of the agency for Technological and Environmental Assessment shall include the following, but not limited thereto:

   a) To establish and maintain a registration and description of all significant technological innovations, together with impact projections.

   b) To examine, analyze and assess the impacts and consequences of technological innovations which may have either significant beneficial or significant harmful or dangerous consequences for human life or for the ecology of life on Earth, or which may require particular regulations or prohibitions to prevent or eliminate dangers or to assure benefits.

   c) To examine, analyze and assess environmental and ecological problems, in particular the environmental and ecological problems which may result from any intrusions or changes of the environment or ecological relationships which may be caused by technological innovations, processes of resource development, patterns of human settlements, the production of energy, patterns of economic and industrial development, or other man-made intrusions and changes of the environment, or which may result from natural causes.

   d) To maintain a global monitoring network to measure possible harmful effects of technological innovations and environmental disturbances so that corrective measures can be designed.

   e) To prepare recommendations based on technological and environmental analyses and assessments, which can serve as guides to the World Parliament, the World Executive, the World Administration, the Agency for Research and Planning, and to the other organs, departments and agencies of the World Government, as well as to individuals in the service of the World Government and to national and local governments and legislative bodies.

   f) To enlist the voluntary or contractual aid and participation of private and public universities, colleges, research institutions and other associations and organizations in the work of technological and environmental assessment.

   g) To enlist the voluntary or contractual aid and participation of private and public universities and colleges, research institutions and other organizations in devising and developing alternatives to harmful or dangerous technologies and environmentally disruptive activities, and in devising controls to assure beneficial results from technological innovations or to prevent harmful results from either technological innovations or environmental changes, all subject to legislation for implementation by the World Parliament.

2. The Agency for Technological and Environmental Assessment shall be supervised by a ten member commission in addition to the Senior Administrator and Cabinet Minister or Vice President. The commission shall be composed of one commissioner from each of ten World Electoral and Administrative Magna-Regions. The persons to serve as commissioners shall be nominated by the House of Counsellors, and then appointed by the World Presidium for five year terms. Commissioners may serve consecutive terms.

SECTION G.   THE WORLD FINANCIAL ADMINISTRATION

1. The functions of the World Financial Administration shall include the following, but not limited thereto:

   a) To establish and operate the procedures for the collection of revenues for the World Government, pursuant to legislation by the World Parliament, inclusive of taxes, globally accounted social and public costs, licenses, fees, revenue sharing arrangements, income derived from supra-national public enterprises or projects or resource developments, and all other sources.

   b) To operate a Planetary Accounting Office, and thereunder to make cost/benefits studies and reports of the functioning and activities of the World Government and of its several organs, departments, branches, bureaus, offices, commissions, institutes, agencies and other parts or projects. In making such studies and reports, account shall be taken not only of direct financial costs and benefits, but also of human, social, environmental, indirect, long-term and other costs and benefits, and of actual or possible hazards and damages. Such studies and reports shall also be designed to uncover any wastes, inefficiencies, misapplications, corruptions, diversions, unnecessary costs, and other possible irregularities.

   c) To make cost/benefit studies and reports at the request of any House or committee of the World Parliament, and of the Presidium, the Executive Cabinet, the World Ombudsmus, the Office of World Attorneys General, the World Supreme Court, or of any administrative department or any agency of the Integrative Complex, as well as upon its own initiative.

d) To operate a Planetary Comptrollers Office and thereunder to supervise the disbursement of the funds of the World Government for all purposes, projects and activities duly authorized by this World Constitution, the World Parliament, the World Executive, and other organs, departments and agencies of the World Government.

e) To establish and operate a Planetary Banking System, making the transition to a common global currency, under the terms of specific legislation passed by the World Parliament.

f) Pursuant to specific legislation enacted by the World Parliament, and in conjunction with the Planetary Banking System, to establish and implement the procedures of a Planetary Monetary and Credit System based upon useful productive capacity and performance, both in goods and services. Such a monetary and credit system shall be designed for use within the Planetary Banking System for the financing of the activities and projects of the World Government, and for all other financial purposes approved by the World Parliament, without requiring the payment of interest on bonds, investments or other claims of financial ownership or debt.

g) To establish criteria for the extension of financial credit based upon such considerations as people available to work, usefulness, cost/benefit accounting, human and social values, environmental health and esthetics, minimizing disparities, integrity, competent management, appropriate technology, potential production and performance.

h) To establish and operate a Planetary Insurance System in areas of world need which transcend national boundaries and in accordance with legislation passed by the World Parliament.

i) To assist the Presidium as may be requested in the technical preparation of budgets for the operation of the World Government.

2. The World Financial Administration shall be supervised by a commission of ten members, together with a Senior Administrator and a Cabinet Minister or Vice President. The commission shall be composed of one commissioner each to be named by the House of Peoples, the House of Nations, the House of Counsellors, the Presidium, the Collegium of World Judges, the Office of Attorneys General, the World Ombudsmus, the Agency for Research and Planning, the Agency for Technological and Environmental Assessment, and the Institute on Governmental Procedures and World Problems. Commissioners shall serve terms of five years, and may serve consecutive terms.

SECTION H.   COMMISSION FOR LEGISLATIVE REVIEW

1. The functions of the Commission for Legislative Review shall be to examine World Legislation and World Laws which the World Parliament enacts or adopts from the previous Body of International Law for the purpose of analyzing whether any particular legislation or law has become obsolete or obstructive or defective in serving the purposes intended; and to make recommendations to the World Parliament accordingly for repeal or amendment or replacement.

2. The Commission for Legislative Review shall be composed of twelve members, including two each to be elected by the House of Peoples, the House of Nations, the House of Counsellors, the Collegium of World Judges, the World Ombudsmus and the Presidium. Members of the Commission shall serve terms of ten years, and may be re-elected to serve consecutive terms. One half of the Commission members after the Commission is first formed shall be elected every five years, with the first terms for one half of the members to be only five years.

ARTICLE IX
THE WORLD JUDICIARY

SECTION A.   JURISDICTION OF THE WORLD SUPREME COURT

1. A World Supreme Court shall be established, together with such regional and district World Courts as may subsequently be found necessary. The World Supreme Court shall comprise a number of benches.

2. The World Supreme Court, together with such regional and district World Courts as may be established, shall have mandatory jurisdiction in all cases, actions, disputes, conflicts, violations of law, civil suits, guarantees of civil and human rights, constitutional interpretations, and other ligitations arising under the provisions of this World Constitution, world legislation, and the body of world law approved by the World Parliament.

3. Decisions of the World Supreme Court shall be binding on all parties involved in all cases, actions and litigations brought before any bench of the World Supreme Court for settlement. Each bench of the World Supreme Court shall constitute a court of highest appeal, except when matters of extra-ordinary public importance are assigned or transferred to the Superior Tribunal of the World Supreme Court, as provided in Section E of Article IX.

SECTION B.   BENCHES OF THE WORLD SUPREME COURT

The benches of the World Supreme Court and their respective jurisdictions shall be as follows:

1. Bench for Human Rights: To deal with issues of human rights arising under the guarantee of civil and human rights provided by Article XII of this World Constitution, and arising in pursuance of the provisions of Article XIII of this World Constitution, and arising otherwise under world legislation and the body of world law approved by the World Parliament.

2. Bench for Criminal Cases: To deal with issues arising from the violation of world laws and world legislation by individuals, corporations, groups and associations, but not issues primarily concerned with human rights.

3. Bench for Civil Cases: To deal with issues involving civil law suits and disputes between individuals, corporations, groups and associations arising under world legislation and world law and the administration thereof.

4. Bench for Constitutional Cases: To deal with the interpretation of the World Constitution and with issues and actions arising in connection with the interpretation of the World Constitution.

5. Bench for International Conflicts: To deal with disputes, conflicts and legal contest arising between or among the nations which have joined in the Federation of Earth.

6. Bench for Public Cases: To deal with issues not under the jurisdiction of another bench arising from conflicts, disputes, civil suits or other legal contests between the World Government and corporations, groups or individuals, or between national governments and corporations, groups or individuals in cases involving world legislation and world law.

7. Appellate Bench: To deal with issues involving world legislation and world law which may be appealed from national courts; and to decide which bench to assign a case or action or litigation when a question or disagreement arises over the proper jurisdiction.

8. Advisory Bench: To give opinions upon request on any legal question arising under world law or world legislation, exclusive of contests or actions involving interpretation of the World Constitution. Advisory opinions may be requested by any House or committee of the World Parliament, by the Presidium, any Administrative Department, the Office of World Attorneys General, the World Ombudsmus, or by any agency of the Integrative Complex.

9. Other benches may be established, combined or terminated upon recommendation of the Collegium of World Judges with approval by the World Parliament; but benches numbers one through eight may not be combined nor terminated except by amendment of this World Constitution.

SECTION C.   SEATS OF THE WORLD SUPREME COURT

1. The primary seat of the World Supreme Court and of all benches shall be the same as for the location of the Primary World Capital and for the location of the World Parliament and the World Executive.

2. Continental seats of the World Supreme Court shall be established in the four secondary capitals of the World Government located in four different Continental Divisions of Earth, as provided in Article XV.

3. The following permanent benches of the World Supreme Court shall be established both at the primary seat and at each of the continental seats: Human Rights, Criminal Cases, Civil Cases, and Public Cases.

4. The following permanent benches of the World Supreme Court shall be located only at the primary seat of the World Supreme Court: Constitutional Cases, International Conflicts, Appellate Bench, and Advisory Bench.

5. Benches which are located permanently only at the primary seat of the World Supreme Court may hold special sessions at the other continental seats of the World Supreme Court when necessary, or may establish continental circuits if needed.

6. Benches of the World Supreme Court which have permanent continental locations may hold special sessions at other locations when needed, or may establish regional circuits if needed.

SECTION D.   THE COLLEGIUM OF WORLD JUDGES

1. A Collegium of World Judges shall be established by the World Parliament. The Collegium shall consist of a minimum of twenty member judges, and may be expanded as needed but not to exceed sixty members.

2. The World Judges to compose the Collegium of World Judges shall be nominated by the House of Counsellors and shall be elected by plurality vote of the three Houses of the World Parliament in joint session. The House of Counsellors shall nominate between two and three times the number of world judges to be elected at any one time. An equal number of World Judges shall be elected from each of ten World Electoral and Administrative Magna-Regions, if not immediately then by rotation.

3. The term of office for a World Judge shall be ten years. Successive terms may be served without limit.

4. The Collegium of World Judges shall elect a Presiding Council of World Judges, consisting of a Chief Justice and four Associate Chief Justices. One member of the Presiding Council of World Judges shall be elected from each of five Continental Divisions of Earth. Members of the Presiding Council of World Judges shall serve five year terms on the Presiding Council, and may serve two successive terms, but not two successive terms as Chief Justice.

5. The Presiding Council of World Judges shall assign all World Judges, including themselves, to the several benches of the World Supreme Court. Each bench for a sitting at each location shall have a minimum of three World Judges, except that the number of World Judges for benches on Constitutional Cases and International Conflicts, and the Appellate Bench, shall be no less than five.

6. The member judges of each bench at each location shall choose annually a Presiding Judge, who may serve two successive terms.

7. The members of the several benches may be reconstituted from time to time as may seem desirable or necessary upon the decision of the Presiding Council of World Judges. Any decision to re-constitute a bench shall be referred to a vote of the entire Collegium of World Judges by request of any World Judge.

8. Any World Judge may be removed from office for cause by an absolute two-thirds majority vote of the three Houses of the World Parliament in joint session.

9. Qualifications for Judges of the World Supreme Court shall be at least ten years of legal or juristic experience, minimum age of thirty years, and evident competence in world law and the humanities.

10. The salaries, expenses, remunerations and prerogatives of the World Judges shall be determined by the World Parliament, and shall be reviewed every five years, but shall not be changed to the disadvantage of any World Judge during a term of office. All members of the Collegium of World Judges shall receive the same salaries, except that additional compensation may be given to the Presiding Council of World Judges.

11. Upon recommendation by the Collegium of World Judges, the World Parliament shall have the authority to establish regional and district world courts below the World Supreme Court, and to establish the jurisdictions thereof, and the procedures for appeal to the World Supreme Court or to the several benches thereof.

12. The detailed rules of procedure for the functioning of the World

Supreme Court, the Collegium of World Judges, and for each bench of the World Supreme Court, shall be decided and amended by absolute majority vote of the Collegium of World Judges.

SECTION E. THE SUPERIOR TRIBUNAL OF THE WORLD SUPREME COURT

1. A Superior Tribunal of the World Supreme Court shall be established to take cases which are considered to be of extra-ordinary public importance. The Superior Tribunal for any calendar year shall consist of the Presiding Council of World Judges together with one World Judge named by the Presiding Judge of each bench of the World Court sitting at the primary seat of the World Supreme Court. The composition of the Superior Tribunal may be continued unchanged for a second year by decision of the Presiding Council of World Judges.

2. Any party to any dispute, issue, case or litigation coming under the jurisdiction of the World Supreme Court, may apply to any particular bench of the World Supreme Court or to the Presiding Council of World Judges for the assignment or transfer of the case to the Superior Tribunal on the grounds of extra-ordinary public importance. If the application is granted, the case shall be heard and disposed of by the Superior Tribunal. Also, any bench taking any particular case, if satisfied that the case is of extra-ordinary public importance, may of its own discretion transfer the case to the Superior Tribunal.

ARTICLE X
THE ENFORCEMENT SYSTEM

SECTION A. BASIC PRINCIPLES

1. The enforcement of world law and world legislation shall apply directly to individuals, and individuals shall be held responsible for compliance with world law and world legislation regardless of whether the individuals are acting in their own capacity or as agents or officials of governments at any level or of the institutions of governments, or as agents or officials of corporations, organizations, associations or groups of any kind.

2. When world law or world legislation or decisions of the world courts are violated, the Enforcement System shall operate to identify and apprehend the individuals responsible for violations.

3. Any enforcement action shall not violate the civil and human rights guaranteed under this World Constitution.

4. The enforcement of world law and world legislation shall be carried out in the context of a non-military world federation wherein all member nations shall disarm as a condition for joining and benefiting from the world federation, subject to Article XVII, Sec. C-8 and D-6. The Federation of Earth and World Government under this World Constitution shall neither keep nor use weapons of mass destruction.

5. Those agents of the enforcement system whose function shall be to apprehend and bring to court violators of world law and world legislation shall be equipped only with such weapons as are appropriate for the apprehension of the individuals responsible for violations.

6. The enforcement of world law and world legislation under this World Constitution shall be conceived and developed primarily as the processes of effective design and administration of world law and world legislation to serve the welfare of all people on Earth, with equity and justice, in which the resources of Earth and the funds and the credits of the World Government are used only to serve peaceful human needs, and none used for weapons of mass destruction or for war-making capabilities.

SECTION B.   THE STRUCTURE FOR ENFORCEMENT

1. The Enforcement System shall be headed by an Office or World Attorneys General and a Commission of Regional World Attorneys.

2. The Office of World Attorneys General shall be composed of five members, one of whom shall be designated as the World Attorney General and the other four shall each be designated an Associate World Attorney General.

3. The Commission of Regional World Attorneys shall consist of twenty Regional World Attorneys.

4. The members to compose the Office of World Attorneys General shall be nominated by the House of Counsellors, with three nominees from each Continental Division of Earth. One member of the Office shall be elected from each of five Continental Divisions by plurality vote of the three houses of the World Parliament in joint session.

5. The term of office for a member of the Office of World Attorneys General shall be ten years. A member may serve two consecutive terms. The position of World Attorney General shall rotate every two years among the five members of the Office. The order of rotation shall be decided among the five members of the Office.

6. The Office of World Attorneys General shall nominate members for the Commission of twenty Regional World Attorneys from the

twenty World Electoral and Administrative Regions, with between two and three nominees submitted for each Region. From these nominations, the three Houses of the World Parliament in joint session shall elect one Regional World Attorney from each of the twenty Regions. Regional World Attorneys shall serve terms of five years, and may serve three consecutive terms.

7. Each Regional World Attorney shall organize and be in charge of an Office of Regional World Attorney. Each Associate World Attorney General shall supervise five Offices of Regional World Attorney.

8. The staff to carry out the work of enforcement, in addition to the five members of the Office of World Attorneys General and the twenty Regional World Attorneys, shall be selected from civil service lists, and shall be organized for the following functions:

   a) Investigation

   b) Apprehension and arrest

   c) Prosecution

   d) Remedies and correction

   e) Conflict resolution

9. Qualifications for a member of the Office of World Attorneys General and for the Regional World Attorneys shall be at least thirty years of age, at least seven years legal experience, and education in law and the humanities.

10. The World Attorney General, the Associate World Attorneys General, and the Regional World Attorneys shall at all times be responsible to the World Parliament. Any member of the Office of World Attorneys General and any Regional World Attorney may be removed from office by a simple majority vote of the three Houses of the World Parliament in joint session.

SECTION C. THE WORLD POLICE

1. That section of the staff of the Office of World Attorneys General and of the Offices of Regional World Attorney responsible for the apprehension and arrest of violators of world law and world legislation, shall be designated as World Police.

2. Each regional staff of the World Police shall be headed by a Regional World Police Captain, who shall be appointed by the Regional World Attorney.

3. The Office of World Attorneys General shall appoint a World Police Supervisor, to be in charge of those activities which transcend regional boundaries. The World Police Supervisor shall direct the

Regional World Police Captains in any actions which require coordinated or joint action transcending regional boundaries, and shall direct any action which requires initiation or direction from the Office of World Attorneys General.

4. Searches and arrests to be made by World Police shall be made only upon warrants issued by the Office of World Attorneys General or by a Regional World Attorney.

5. World Police shall be armed only with weapons appropriate for the apprehension of the individuals responsible for violation of world law.

6. Employment in the capacity of World Police Captain and World Police Supervisor shall be limited to ten years.

7. The World Police Supervisor and any Regional World Police Captain may be removed from office for cause by decision of the Office of World Attorneys General or by absolute majority vote of the three Houses of the World Parliament in joint session.

SECTION D.   MEANS OF ENFORCEMENT

1. Non-military means of enforcement of world law and world legislation shall be developed by the World Parliament and by the Office of World Attorneys General in consultation with the Commission of Regional World Attorneys, the Collegium of World Judges, the World Presidium, and the World Ombudsmus. The actual means of enforcement shall require legislation by the World Parliament.

2. Non-military means of enforcement which can be developed may include: Denial of financial credit; denial of material resources and personnel; revocation of licenses, charters, or corporate rights; impounding of equipment; fines and damage payments; performance of work to rectify damages; imprisonment or isolation; and other means appropriate to the specific situations.

3. To cope with situations of potential or actual riots, insurrection and resort to armed violence, particular strategies and methods shall be developed by the World Parliament and by the Office of World Attorneys General in consultation with the Commission of Regional World Attorneys, the collegium of World Judges, the Presidium and the World Ombudsmus. Such strategies and methods shall require enabling legislation by the World Parliament where required in addition to the specific provisions of this World Constitution.

4. A basic condition for preventing outbreaks of violence which the Enforcement System shall facilitate in every way possible, shall be to assure a fair hearing under non-violent circumstances for any person

or group having a grievance, and likewise to assure a fair opportunity for a just settlement of any grievance with due regard for the rights and welfare of all concerned.

ARTICLE XI
THE WORLD OMBUDSMUS

SECTION A. FUNCTIONS AND POWERS OF
THE WORLD OMBUDSMUS

The functions and powers of the World Ombudsmus, as public defender, shall include the following:

1. To protect the People of Earth and all individuals against violations or neglect of universal human and civil rights which are stipulated in Article XII and other sections of this World Constitution.

2. To protect the People of Earth against violations of this World Constitution by any official or agency of the World Government, including both elected and appointed officials or public employees regardless of organ, department, office, agency or rank.

3. To press for the implementation of the Directive Principles for the World Government as defined in Article XIII of this World Constitution.

4. To promote the welfare of the people of Earth by seeking to assure that conditions of social justice and of minimizing disparities are achieved in the implementation and administration of world legislation and world law.

5. To keep on the alert for perils to humanity arising from technological innovations, environmental disruptions and other diverse sources, and to launch initiatives for correction or prevention of such perils.

6. To ascertain that the administration of otherwise proper laws, ordinances and procedures of the World Government do not result in unforseen injustices or inequities, or become stultified in bureaucracy or the details of administration.

7. To receive and hear complaints, grievances or requests for aid from any person, group, organization, association, body politic or agency concerning any matter which comes within the purview of the World Ombudsmus.

8. To request the Office of World Attorneys General or any Regional World Attorney to initiate legal actions or court proceedings whenever and wherever considered necessary or desirable in the view of the World Ombudsmus.

9. To directly initiate legal actions and court proceedings whenever the World Ombudsmus deems necessary.

10. To review the functioning of the departments, bureaus, offices, commissions, institutes, organs and agencies of the World Government to ascertain whether the procedures of the World Government are adequately fulfilling their purposes and serving the welfare of humanity in optimum fashion, and to make recommendations for improvements.

11. To present an annual report to the World Parliament and to the Presidium on the activities of the World Ombudsmus, together with any recommendations for legislative measures to improve the functioning of the World Government for the purpose of better serving the welfare of the People of Earth.

SECTION B. COMPOSITION OF THE WORLD OMBUDSMUS

1. The World Ombudsmus shall be headed by a Council of World Ombudsmen of five members, one of whom shall be designated as Principal World Ombudsman, while the other four shall each be designated as an Associate World Ombudsman.

2. Members to compose the Council of World Ombudsmen shall be nominated by the House of Counsellors, with three nominees from each Continental Division of Earth. One member of the Council shall be elected from each of five Continental Divisions by plurality vote of the three Houses of the World Parliament in joint session.

3. The term of office for a World Ombudsman shall be ten years. A World Ombudsman may serve two successive terms. The position of Principal World Ombudsman shall be rotated every two years. The order of rotation shall be determined by the Council of World Ombudsmen.

4. The Council of World Ombudsmen shall be assisted by a Commission of World Advocates of twenty members. Members for the Commission of World Advocates shall be nominated by the Council of World Ombudsmen from twenty World Electoral and Administrative Regions, with between two and three nominees submitted for each Region. One World Advocate shall be elected from each of the twenty World Electoral and Administrative Regions by the three Houses of the World Parliament in joint session. World Advocates shall serve terms of five years, and may serve a maximum of four successive terms.

5. The Council of World Ombudsmen shall establish twenty regional offices, in addition to the principal world office at the primary seat of

the World Government. The twenty regional offices of the World Ombudsmus shall parallel the organization of the twenty Offices of Regional World Attorney.

6. Each regional office of the World Ombudsmus shall be headed by a World Advocate. Each five regional offices of the World Ombudsmus shall be supervised by an Associate World Ombudsman.

7. Any World Ombudsman and any World Advocate may be removed from office for cause by an absolute majority vote of the three Houses of the World Parliament in joint session.

8. Staff members for the World Ombudsmus and for each regional office of the World Ombudsmus shall be selected and employed from civil service lists.

9. Qualifications for Ombudsman and for World Advocate shall be at least thirty years of age, at least five years legal experience, and education in law and other relevant education.

ARTICLE XII
BILL OF RIGHTS FOR THE CITIZENS OF EARTH

The inhabitants and citizens of Earth who are within the Federation of Earth shall have certain inalienable rights defined hereunder. It shall be mandatory for the World Parliament, the World Executive, and all organs and agencies of the World Government to honor, implement and enforce these rights, as well as for the national governments of all member nations in the Federation of Earth to do likewise. Individuals or groups suffering violation or neglect of such rights shall have full recourse through the World Ombudsmus, the Enforcement System and the World Courts for redress of grievances. The inalienable rights shall include the following:

1. Equal rights for all citizens of the Federation of Earth, with no discrimination on grounds of race, color, caste, nationality, sex, religion, political affiliation, property, or social status.

2. Equal protection and application of world legislation and world laws for all citizens of the Federation of Earth.

3. Freedom of thought and conscience, speech, press, writing, communication, expression, publication, broadcasting, telecasting, and cinema, except as an overt part of or incitement to violence, armed riot or insurrection.

4. Freedom of assembly, association, organization, petition and peaceful demonstration.

5. Freedom to vote without duress, and freedom for political organization and campaigning without censorship or recrimination.

6. Freedom to profess, practice and promote religious or religious beliefs or no religion or religious belief.

7. Freedom to profess and promote political beliefs or no political beliefs.

8. Freedom for investigation, research and reporting.

9. Freedom to travel without passport or visas or other forms of registration used to limit travel between, among or within nations.

10. Prohibition against slavery, peonage, involuntary servitude, and conscription of labor.

11. Prohibition against military conscription.

12. Safety of person from arbitrary or unreasonable arrest, detention, exile, search of seizure; requirement of warrants for searches and arrests.

13. Prohibition against physical or psychological duress or torture during any period of investigation, arrest, detention or imprisonment, and against cruel or unusual punishment.

14. Right of habeas corpus; no ex-post-facto laws; no double jeopardy; right to refuse self-incrimination or the incrimination of another.

15. Prohibition against private armies and paramilitary organizations as being threats to the common peace and safety.

16. Safety of property from arbitrary seizure; protection against exercise of the power of eminent domain without reasonable compensation.

17. Right to family planning and free public assistance to achieve family planning objectives.

18. Right of privacy of person, family and association; prohibition against surveillance as a means of political control.

ARTICLE XIII
DIRECTIVE PRINCIPLES FOR THE WORLD GOVERNMENT

It shall be the aim of the World Government to secure certain other rights for all inhabitants within the Federation of Earth, but without immediate guarantee of universal achievement and enforcement. These rights are defined as Directive Principles, obligating the World Government to pursue every reasonable means for universal realization and implementation, and shall include the following:

1. Equal opportunity for useful employment for everyone, with wages or remuneration sufficient to assure human dignity.

2. Freedom of choice in work, occupation, employment or profession.

3. Full access to information and to the accumulated knowledge of the human race.

4. Free and adequate public education available to everyone, extending to the pre-university level; equal opportunities for elementary and higher education for all persons; equal opportunity for continued education for all persons throughout life; the right of any person or parent to choose a private educational institution at any time.

5. Free and adequate public health services and medical care available to everyone throughout life under conditions of free choice.

6. Equal opportunity for leisure time for everyone; better distribution of the work load of society so that every person may have equitable leisure time opportunities.

7. Equal opportunity for everyone to enjoy the benefits of scientific and technological discoveries and developments.

8. Protection for everyone against the hazards and perils of technological innovations and developments.

9. Protection of the natural environment which is the common heritage of humanity against pollution, ecological disruption or damage which could imperil life or lower the quality of life.

10. Conservation of those natural resources of Earth which are limited so that present and future generations may continue to enjoy life on the planet Earth.

11. Assurance for everyone of adequate housing, of adequate and nutritious food supplies, of safe and adequate water supplies, of pure air with protection of oxygen supplies and the ozone layer, and in general for the continuance of an environment which can sustain healthy living for all.

12. Assure to each child the right to the full realization of his or her potential.

13. Social Security for everyone to relieve the hazards of unemployment, sickness, old age, family circumstance, disability, catastrophies of nature, and technological change, and to allow retirement with sufficient lifetime income for living under conditions of human dignity during older age.

14. Rapid elimination of and prohibitions against technological hazards and man-made environmental disturbances which are found to create dangers to life on Earth.

15. Implementation of intensive programs to discover, develop and institute safe alternatives and practical substitutions for technologies which must be eliminated and prohibited because of hazards and dangers to life.

16. Encouragement for cultural diversity; encouragement for decentralized administration.

17. Freedom for peaceful self-determination for minorities, refugees and dissenters.

18. Freedom for change of residence to anywhere on Earth conditioned by provisions for temporary sanctuaries in events of large numbers of refugees, stateless persons, or mass migrations.

19. Prohibition against the death penalty.

ARTICLE XIV
SAFEGUARDS AND RESERVATIONS

SECTION A.   CERTAIN SAFEGUARDS

The World Government shall operate to secure for all nations and peoples within the Federation of Earth the safeguards which are defined hereunder:

1. Guarantee that full faith and credit shall be given to the public acts, records, legislation and judicial proceedings of the member nations within the Federation of Earth, consistent with the several provisions of this World Constitution.

2. Assure freedom of choice within the member nations and countries of the Federation of Earth to determine their internal political, economic and social systems, consistent with the guarantees and protections given under this World Constitution to assure civil liberties and human rights and a safe environment for life, and otherwise consistent with the several provisions of this World Constitution.

3. Grant the right of asylum within the Federation of Earth for persons who may seek refuge from countries or nations which are not yet included within the Federation of Earth.

4. Grant the right of individuals and groups, after the Federation of Earth includes 90 percent of the territory of Earth, to peacefully leave the hegemony of the Federation of Earth and to live in suitable territory set aside by the Federation neither restricted nor protected by the World Government, provided that such territory does not extend beyond five percent of Earth's habitable territory, is kept completely disarmed and not used as a base for inciting violence or insurrection within or against the Federation of Earth or any member nation, and is kept free of acts of environmental or technological damage which seriously affect Earth outside such territory.

SECTION B.   RESERVATION OF POWERS

The powers not delegated to the World Government by this World Constitution shall be reserved to the nations of the Federation of Earth and to the people of Earth.

ARTICLE XV
WORLD FEDERAL ZONES AND THE WORLD CAPITALS

SECTION A. WORLD FEDERAL ZONES

1. Twenty World Federal Zones shall be established within the twenty World Electoral and Administrative Regions, for the purpose of the location of the several organs of the World Government and of the administrative departments, the world courts, the offices of the Regional World Attorneys, the offices of the World Advocates, and for the location of other branches, departments, institutes, offices, bureaus, commissions, agencies and parts of the World Government.

2. The World Federal Zones shall be established as the needs and resources of the World Government develop and expand. World Federal Zones shall be established first within each of five Continental Divisions.

3. The location and administration of the World Federal Zones, including the first five, shall be determined by the World Parliament.

SECTION B. THE WORLD CAPITALS

1. Five World Capitals shall be established in each of five Continental Divisions of Earth, to be located in each of the five World Federal Zones which are established first as provided in Article XV of this World Constitution.

2. One of the World Capitals shall be designated by the World Parliament as the Primary World Capital, and the other four shall be designated as Secondary World Capitals.

3. The primary seats of all organs of the World Government shall be located in the Primary World Capital, and other major seats of the several organs of the World Government shall be located in the Secondary World Capitals.

SECTION C. LOCATIONAL PROCEDURES

1. Choices for location of the twenty World Federal Zones and for the five World Capitals shall be proposed by the Presidium, and then shall be decided by a simple majority vote of the three Houses of the World Parliament in joint session. The Presidium shall offer choices of two or three locations in each of the twenty World Electoral and Administrative Regions to be World Federal Zones, and shall offer two alternative choices for each of the five World Capitals.

2. The Presidium in consultation with the Executive Cabinet shall then

propose which of the five World Capitals shall be the Primary World Capital, to be decided by a simple majority vote of the three Houses of the World Parliament in joint session.

3. Each organ of the World Government shall decide how best to apportion and organize its functions and activities among the five World Capitals, and among the twenty World Federal Zones, subject to specific directions from the World Parliament.

4. The World Parliament may decide to rotate its sessions among the five World Capitals, and if so, to decide the procedure for rotation.

5. For the first two operative stages of World Government as defined in Article XVII, and for the Provisional World Government as defined in Article XIX, a provisional location may be selected for the Primary World Capital. The provisional location need not be continued as a permanent location.

6. Any World Capital or World Federal Zone may be relocated by an absolute two-thirds majority vote of the three Houses of the World Parliament in joint session.

7. Additional World Federal Zones may be designated if found necessary by proposal of the Presidium and approval by an absolute majority vote of the three Houses of the World Parliament in joint session.

ARTICLE XVI
WORLD TERRITORY AND EXTERIOR RELATIONS

SECTION A.   WORLD TERRITORY

1. Those areas of the Earth and Earth's moon which are not under the jurisdiction of existing nations at the time of forming the Federation of Earth, or which are not reasonably within the province of national ownership and administration, or which are declared to be World Territory subsequent to establishment of the Federation of Earth, shall be designated as World Territory and shall belong to all of the people of Earth.

2. The administration of World Territory shall be determined by the World Parliament and implemented by the World Executive, and shall apply to the following areas:

   a) All oceans and seas having an international or supra-national character, together with the seabeds and resources thereof, beginning at a distance of twenty kilometers offshore, excluding inland seas of traditional nation ownership.

b) Vital straits, channels, and canals.

c) The atmosphere enveloping the Earth, beginning at an elevation of one kilometer above the general surface of the land, excluding the depressions in areas of much variation in elevation.

d) Man-made satellites and Earth's moon.

e) Colonies which may choose the status of World Territory; non-independent territories under the trust administration of nations or of the United Nations; any islands or atolls which are unclaimed by any nation; independent lands or countries which choose the status of World Territory; and disputed lands which choose the status of World Territory.

3. The residents of any World Territory, except designated World Federal Zones, shall have the right within reason to decide by plebiscite to become a self-governing nation within the Federation of Earth, either singly or in combination with other World Territories, or to unite with an existing nation within the Federation of Earth.

SECTION B. EXTERIOR RELATIONS

1. The World Government shall maintain exterior relations with those nations of Earth which have not joined the Federation of Earth. Exterior relations shall be under the administration of the Presidium, subject at all times to specific instructions and approval by the World Parliament.

2. All treaties and agreements with nations remaining outside the Federation of Earth shall be negotiated by the Presidium and must be ratified by a simple majority vote of the three Houses of the Parliament.

3. The World Government for the Federation of Earth shall establish and maintain peaceful relations with other planets and celestial bodies where and when it may become possible to establish communications with the possible inhabitants thereof.

4. All explorations into outer space, both within and beyond the solar system in which Planet Earth is located, shall be under the exclusive direction and control of the World Government, and shall be conducted in such manner as shall be determined by the World Parliament.

ARTICLE XVII
RATIFICATION AND IMPLEMENTATION

SECTION A.   RATIFICATION OF THE WORLD CONSTITUTION

This World Constitution shall be submitted to the nations and people of Earth for ratification by the following procedures:

1. The World Constitution shall be transmitted to the General Assembly of the United Nations Organization and to each national government on Earth, with the request that the World Constitution be submitted to the national legislature of each nation for preliminary ratification and to the people of each nation for final ratification by popular referendum.

2. Preliminary ratification by a national legislature shall be accomplished by simple majority vote of the national legislature.

3. Final ratification by the people shall be accomplished by a simple majority of votes cast in a popular referendum, provided that a minimum of twenty-five percent of eligible voters of age eighteen years and over have cast ballots within the nation or country or within World Electoral and Administrative Districts.

4. In the case of a nation without a national legislature, the head of the national government shall be requested to give preliminary ratification and to submit the World Constitution for final ratification by popular referendum.

5. In the event that a national government, after six months, fails to submit the World Constitution for ratification as requested, then the global agency assuming responsibility for the worldwide ratification campaign may proceed to conduct a direct referendum for ratification of the World Constitution by the people. Direct referendums may be organized on the basis of entire nations or countries, or on the basis of existing defined communities within nations.

6. In the event of a direct ratification referendum, final ratification shall be accomplished by a majority of the votes cast whether for an entire nation or for a World Electoral and Administrative District, provided that ballots are cast by a minimum of twenty-five percent of eligible voters of the area who are over eighteen years of age.

7. For ratification by existing communities within a nation, the procedure shall be to request local communities, cities, counties, states, provinces, cantons, prefectures, tribal jurisdictions, or other defined political units within a nation to ratify the World Constitution, and to submit the World Constitution for a referendum vote by the citizens of the community or political unit. Ratification may be

accomplished by proceeding in this way until all eligible voters of age eighteen and above within the nation or World Electoral and Administrative District have had the opportunity to vote, provided that ballots are cast by a minimum of twenty-five percent of those eligible to vote.

8. Prior to the Full Operative Stage of World Government, as defined under Section E of Article XVII, the universities, colleges and scientific academies and institutes in any country may ratify the World Constitution, thus qualifying them for participation in the nomination of Members of the World Parliament to the House of Counsellors.

9. In the case of those nations currently involved in serious international disputes or where traditional enmities and chronic disputes may exist among two or more nations, a procedure for concurrent paired ratification shall be instituted whereby the nations which are parties to a current or chronic international dispute or conflict may simultaneously ratify the World Constitution. In such cases, the paired nations shall be admitted into the Federation of Earth simultaneously, with the obligation for each such nation to immediately turn over all weapons of mass destruction to the World Government, and to turn over the conflict or dispute for mandatory peaceful settlement by the World Government.

10. Each nation or political unit which ratifies this World Constitution, either by preliminary ratification or final ratification, shall be bound never to use any armed forces or weapons of mass destruction against another member or unit of the Federation of Earth, regardless of how long it may take to achieve full disarmament of all the nations and political units which ratify this World Constitution.

11. When ratified, the Constitution for the Federation of Earth becomes the supreme law of Earth. By the act of ratifying this Earth Constitution, any provision in the Constitution or Legislation of any country so ratifying, which is contrary to this Earth Constitution, is either repealed or amended to conform with the Constitution for the Federation of Earth, effective as soon as 25 countries have so ratified. The amendment of National or State Constitutions to allow entry into World Federation is not necessary prior to ratification of the Constitution for the Federation of Earth.

SECTION B.   STAGES OF IMPLEMENTATION

1. Implementation of this World Constitution and the establishment of World Government pursuant to the terms of this World Constitution, may be accomplished in three stages, as follows, in addition to

the stage of a Provisional World Government as provided under Article XIX:

a) First Operative Stage of World Government

b) Second Operative Stage of World Government

c) Full Operative Stage of World Government

2. At the beginning and during each stage, the World Parliament and the World Executive together shall establish goals and develop means for the progressive implementation of the World Constitution, and for the implementation of legislation enacted by the World Parliament.

SECTION C. FIRST OPERATIVE STAGE OF WORLD GOVERNMENT

1. The first operative stage of World Government under this World Constitution shall be implemented when the World Constitution is ratified by a sufficient number of nations and/or people to meet one or the other of the following conditions or equivalent:

   a) Preliminary or final ratification by a minimum of twenty-five nations, each having a population of more than 100,000.

   b) Preliminary or final ratification by a minimum of ten nations above 100,000 population, together with ratification by direct referendum within a minimum of fifty additional World Electoral and Administrative Districts.

   c) Ratification by direct referendum within a minimum of 100 World Electoral and Administrative Districts, even though no nation as such has ratified.

2. The election of Members of the World Parliament to the House of Peoples shall be conducted in all World Electoral and Administrative Districts where ratification has been accomplished by popular referendum.

3. The Election of Members of the World Parliament to the House of Peoples may proceed concurrently with direct popular referendums both prior to and after the First Operative Stage of World Government is reached.

4. The appointment or election of Members of the World Parliament to the House of Nations shall proceed in all nations where preliminary ratification has been accomplished.

5. One-fourth of the Members of the World Parliament of the House of Counsellors may be elected from nominees submitted by universities and colleges which have ratified the World Constitution.

6. The World Presidium and the Executive Cabinet shall be elected according to the provisions in Article VI, except that in the absence

of a House of Counsellors, the nominations shall be made by the members of the House of Peoples and of the House of Nations in joint session. Until this is accomplished, the Presidium and Executive Cabinet of the Provisional World Government as provided in Article XIX, shall continue to serve.

7. When composed, the Presidium for the first operative stage of World Government shall assign or re-assign Ministerial posts among Cabinet and Presidium members, and shall immediately establish or confirm a World Disarmament Agency and a World Economic and Development Organization.

8. Those nations which ratify this World Constitution and thereby join the Federation of Earth, shall immediately transfer all weapons of mass destruction as defined and designated by the World Disarmament Agency to that Agency. (See Article XIX, Sections A-2-d, B-6 and E-5). The World Disarmament Agency shall immediately immobilize all such weapons and shall proceed with dispatch to dismantle, convert to peacetime use, re-cycle the materials thereof or otherwise destroy all such weapons. During the first operative stage of World Government, the ratifying nations may retain armed forces equipped with weapons other than weapons of mass destruction as defined and designated by the World Disarmament Agency.

9. Concurrently with the reduction or elimination of such weapons of mass destruction and other military expenditures as can be accomplished during the first operative stage of World Government, the member nations of the Federation of Earth shall pay annually to the Treasury of the World Government amounts equal to one-half the amounts saved from their respective national military budgets during the last year before joining the Federation, and shall continue such payments until the full operative stage of World Government is reached. The World Government shall use fifty percent of the funds thus received to finance the work and projects of the World Economic Development Organization.

10. The World Parliament and the World Executive shall continue to develop the organs, departments, agencies and activities originated under the Provisional World Government, with such amendments as deemed necessary; and shall proceed to establish and begin the following organs, departments and agencies of the World Government, if not already underway, together with such other departments, and agencies as are considered desirable and feasible during the first operative stage of World Government:

a) The World Supreme Court;

b) The Enforcement System;

c) The World Ombudsmus;

d) The World Civil Service Administration;

e) The World Financial Administration;

f) The Agency for Research and Planning;

g) The Agency for Technological and Environmental Assessment;

h) An Emergency Earth Rescue Administration, concerned with all aspects of climate change and related factors;

i) An Integrated Global Energy System, based on environmentally safe sources;

j) A World University System, under the Department of Education;

k) A World Corporations Office, under the Department of Commerce and Industry;

l) The World Service Corps;

m) A World Oceans and Seabeds Administration.

11. At the beginning of the first operative stage, the Presidium in consultation with the Executive Cabinet shall formulate and put forward a proposed program for solving the most urgent world problems currently confronting humanity.

12. The World Parliament shall proceed to work upon solutions to world problems. The World Parliament and the World Executive working together shall institute through the several organs, departments and agencies of the World Government whatever means shall seem appropriate and feasible to accomplish the implementation and enforcement of world legislation, world law and the World Constitution; and in particular shall take certain decisive actions for the welfare of all people on Earth, applicable throughout the world, including but not limited to the following:

a) Expedite the organization and work of the Emergency Earth Rescue Administration, concerned with all aspects of climate change and climate crises;

b) Expedite the new finance, credit and monetary system, to serve human needs;

c) Expedite an integrated global energy system, utilizing solar energy, hydrogen energy, and other safe and sustainable sources of energy;

d) Push forward a global program for agricultural production to achieve maximum sustained yield under conditions which are ecologically sound;

e) Establish conditions for free trade within the Federation of Earth;

f) Call for and find ways to implement a moratorium on nuclear energy projects until all problems are solved concerning safety, disposal of toxic wastes and the dangers of use or diversion of materials for the production of nuclear weapons;

g) Outlaw and find ways to completely terminate the production of nuclear weapons and all weapons of mass destruction;

h) Push forward programs to assure adequate and non-polluted water supplies, and clean air supplies for everybody on Earth;

i) Push forward a global program to conserve and re-cycle the resources of Earth.

j) Develop an acceptable program to bring population growth under control, especially by raising standards of living.

SECTION D.   SECOND OPERATIVE STAGE OF WORLD GOVERNMENT

1. The second operative stage of World Government shall be implemented when fifty percent or more of the nations of Earth have given either preliminary or final ratification to this World Constitution, provided that fifty percent of the total population of Earth is included either within the ratifying nations or within the ratifying nations together with additional World Electoral and Administrative Districts where people have ratified the World Constitution by direct referendum.

2. The election and appointment of Members of the World Parliament to the several Houses of the World Parliament shall proceed in the same manner as specified for the first operative stage in Section C-2, 3, 4, and 5 of Article XVII.

3. The terms of office of the Members of the World Parliament elected or appointed for the first operative stage of World Government, shall be extended into the second operative stage unless they have already served five year terms, in which case new elections or appointments shall be arranged. The terms of holdover Members of the World Parliament into the second operative stage shall be adjusted to run concurrently with the terms of those who are newly elected at the beginning of the second operative stage.

4. The World Presidium and the Executive Cabinet shall be reconstituted or reconfirmed, as needed, at the beginning of the second operative stage of World Government.

5. The World Parliament and the World Executive shall continue to develop the organs, departments, agencies and activities which are already underway from the first operative stage of World Govern-

ment, with such amendments as deemed necessary; and shall proceed to establish and develop all other organs and major departments and agencies of the World Government to the extent deemed feasible during the second operative stage.

6. All nations joining the Federation of Earth to compose the second operative stage of World Government, shall immediately transfer all weapons of mass destruction and all other military weapons and equipment to the World Disarmament Agency, which shall immediately immobilize such weapons and equipment and shall proceed forthwith to dismantle, convert to peacetime uses, recycle the materials thereof, or otherwise destroy such weapons and equipment. During the second operative stage, all armed forces and paramilitary forces of the nations which have joined the Federation of Earth shall be completely disarmed and either disbanded or converted on a voluntary basis into elements of the non-military World Service Corps.

7. Concurrently with the reduction or elimination of such weapons, equipment and other military expenditures as can be accomplished during the second operative stage of World Government, the member nations of the Federation of Earth shall pay annually to the Treasury of the World Government amount equal to one-half of the amounts saved from their national military budgets during the last year before joining the Federation and shall continue such payments until the full operative stage of World Government is reached. The World Government shall use fifty percent of the funds thus received to finance the work and projects of the World Economic Development Organization.

8. Upon formation of the Executive Cabinet for the second operative stage, the Presidium shall issue an invitation to the General Assembly of the United Nations Organization and to each of the specialized agencies of the United Nations, as well as to other useful international agencies, to transfer personnel, facilities, equipment, resources and allegiance to the Federation of Earth and to the World Government thereof. The agencies and functions of the United Nations Organization and of its specialized agencies and of other international agencies which may be thus transferred, shall be reconstituted as needed and integrated into the several organs, departments, offices and agencies of the World Government.

9. Near the beginning of the second operative stage, the Presidium in consultation with the Executive cabinet, shall formulate and put forward a proposed program for solving the most urgent world problems currently confronting the people of Earth.

10. The World Parliament shall proceed with legislation necessary for

implementing a complete program for solving the current urgent world problems.

11. The World Parliament and the World Executive working together shall develop through the several organs, departments and agencies of the World Government whatever means shall seem appropriate and feasible to implement legislation for solving world problems; and in particular shall take certain decisive actions for the welfare of all people on Earth, including but not limited to the following:

  a) Declare all oceans, seas and canals having a supra-national character (but not including inland seas traditionally belonging to particular nations) from twenty kilometers offshore, and all the seabeds thereof, to be under the ownership of the Federation of Earth as the common heritage of humanity, and subject to the control and management of the World Government.

  b) Declare the polar caps and surrounding polar areas, including the continent of Antartica but not areas which are traditionally a part of particular nations, to be world territory owned by the Federation of Earth as the common heritage of humanity, and subject to control and management by the World Government.

  c) Outlaw the possession, stockpiling, sale and use of all nuclear weapons, all weapons of mass destruction, and all other military weapons and equipment.

  d) Establish an ever-normal grainery and food supply system for the people of Earth.

  e) Develop and carry forward as feasible all actions defined under Sec. C-10 and C-12 of the First Operative Stage.

SECTION E.   FULL OPERATIVE STAGE OF WORLD GOVERNMENT

1. The full operative stage of World Government shall be implemented when this World Constitution is given either preliminary or final ratification by meeting either condition (a) or (b):

  a) Ratification by eighty percent or more of the nations of Earth comprising at least ninety percent of the population of Earth; or

  b) Ratification which includes ninety percent of Earth's total population, either within ratifying nations or within ratifying nations together with additional World Electoral and Administrative Districts where ratification by direct referendum has been accomplished, as provided in Article XVII, Section A.

2. When the full operative stage of World Government is reached, the following conditions shall be implemented:

a) Elections for Members of the House of Peoples shall be conducted in all World Electoral and Administrative Districts where elections have not already taken place; and Members of the House of Nations shall be elected or appointed by the national legislatures or national governments in all nations where this has not already been accomplished.

b) The terms of office for Members of the House of Peoples and of the House of Nations serving during the second operative stage, shall be continued into the full operative stage, except for those who have already served five years, in which case elections shall be held or appointments made as required.

c) The terms of office for all holdover Members of the House of Peoples and of the House of Nations who have served less than five years, shall be adjusted to run concurrently with those Members of the World Parliament whose terms are beginning with the full operative stage.

d) The second 100 Members of the House of Counsellors shall be elected according to the procedure specified in Section E of Article V. The terms of office for holdover Members of the House of Counsellors shall run five more years after the beginning of the full operative stage, while those beginning their terms with the full operative stage shall serve ten years.

e) The Presidium and the Executive Cabinet shall be reconstituted in accordance with the provisions of Article VI.

f) All organs of the World Government shall be made fully operative, and shall be fully developed for the effective administration and implementation of world legislation, world law and the provisions of this World constitution.

g) All nations which have not already done so shall immediately transfer all military weapons and equipment to the World Disarmament Agency, which shall immediately immobilize all such weapons and shall proceed forthwith to dismantle, convert to peaceful usage, recycle the materials thereof, or otherwise to destroy such weapons and equipment.

h) All armies and military forces of every kind shall be completely disarmed, and either disbanded or converted and integrated on a voluntary basis into the non-military World Service Corps.

i) All viable agencies of the United Nations Organization and other viable international agencies established among national governments, together with their personnel, facilities and resources, shall be transferred to the World Government and reconstituted and integrated as may be useful into the organs, departments, offices, institutes, commissions, bureaus and agencies of the World Government.

j) The World Parliament and the World Executive shall continue to develop the activities and projects which are already underway from the second operative stage of World Government, with such amendments as deemed necessary; and shall proceed with a complete and full-scale program to solve world problems and serve the welfare of all people on Earth, in accordance with the provisions of this World Constitution.

SECTION F. COSTS OF RATIFICATION

The work and costs of private Citizens of Earth for the achievement of a ratified Constitution for the Federation of Earth, are recognized as legitimate costs for the establishment of constitutional world government by which present and future generations will benefit, and shall be repaid double the original amount by the World Financial Administration of the World Government when it becomes operational after 25 countries have ratified this Constitution for the Federation of Earth. Repayment specifically includes contributions to the World Government Funding Corporation and other costs and expenses recognized by standards and procedures to be established by the World Financial Administration.

ARTICLE XVIII
AMENDMENTS

1. Following completion of the first operative stage of World Government, amendments to this World Constitution may be proposed for consideration in two ways:

   a) By a simple majority vote of any House of the World Parliament.

   b) By petitions signed by a total of 200,000 persons eligible to vote in world elections from a total of at least twenty World Electoral and Administrative Districts where the World Constitution has received final ratification.

2. Passage of any amendment proposed by a House of the World Parliament shall require an absolute two-thirds majority vote of each of the three Houses of the World Parliament voting separately.

3. An amendment proposed by popular petition shall first require a simple majority vote of the House of Peoples, which shall be obliged to take a vote upon the proposed amendment. Passage of the amendment shall then require an absolute two-thirds majority vote of each of the three Houses of the World Parliament voting separately.

4. Periodically, but no later than ten years after first convening the World Parliament, for the First Operative Stage of World Government, and every 20 years thereafter, the Members of the World Parliament shall meet in special session comprising a Constitutional Convention to conduct a review of this World Constitution to consider and propose possible amendments, which shall then require action as specified in Clause 2 of Article XVIII for passage.

5. If the First Operative Stage of World Government is not reached by the year 1995, then the Provisional World Parliament, as provided under Article XIX, may convene another session of the World Constituent Assembly to review the Constitution for the Federation of Earth and consider possible amendments according to procedure established by the Provisional World Parliament.

6. Except by the following the amendment procedures specified herein, no part of this World Constitution may be set aside, suspended or subverted, neither for emergencies nor caprice nor convenience.

ARTICLE XIX
PROVISIONAL WORLD GOVERNMENT

SECTION A.   ACTIONS TO BE TAKEN BY THE WORLD CONSTITUENT ASSEMBLY

Upon adoption of the World Constitution by the World Constituent Assembly, the Assembly and such continuing agency or agencies as it shall designate shall do the following, without being limited thereto:

1. Issue a Call to all Nations, communities and people of Earth to ratify this World Constitution for World Government.

2. Establish the following preparatory commissions:

   a) Ratification Commission

   b) World Elections Commission

   c) World Development Commission

   d) World Disarmament Commission

   e) World Problems Commission

   f) Nominating Commission

   g) Finance Commission

   h) Peace Research and Education Commission

   i) Special commissions on each of several of the most urgent world problems

   j) Such other commissions as may be deemed desirable in order to proceed with the Provisional World Government

3. Convene Sessions of a Provisional World Parliament when feasible under the following conditions:

   a) Seek the commitment of 500 or more delegates to attend, representing people in 20 countries from five continents, and having credentials defined by Article XIX, Section C;

   b) The minimum funds necessary to organize the sessions of the Provisional World Parliament are either on hand or firmly pledged.

   c) Suitable locations are confirmed at least nine months in advance, unless emergency conditions justify shorter advance notice.

SECTION B.   WORK OF THE PREPARATORY COMMISSIONS

1. The Ratification Commission shall carry out a worldwide campaign for the ratification of the World Constitution, both to obtain preliminary ratification by national governments, including national legislatures, and to obtain final ratification by people, including communities. The ratification commission shall continue its work until the full operative stage of World Government is reached.

2. The World Elections Commission shall prepare a provisional global map of World Electoral and Administrative Districts and Regions which may be revised during the first or second operative stage of World Government; and shall prepare and proceed with plans to obtain the election of Members of the World Parliament to the House of Peoples and to the House of Counsellors. The World Elections Commission shall in due course be converted into the World Boundaries and Elections Administration.

3. After six months, in those countries where national governments have not responded favorable to the ratification call, the Ratification Commission and the World Elections Commission may proceed jointly to accomplish both the ratification of the World Constitution by direct popular referendum and concurrently the election of Members of the World Parliament.

4. The Ratification Commission may also submit the World Constitution for ratification by universities and colleges throughout the world.

5. The World Development Commission shall prepare plans for the creation of a World Economic Development Organization to serve all nations and people ratifying the World Constitution, and in particular less developed countries to begin functioning when the Provisional World Government is established.

6. The World Disarmament Commission shall prepare plans for the

organization of a World Disarmament Agency, to begin functioning when the Provisional World Government is established.

7. The World Problems Commission shall prepare an agenda of urgent world problems, with documentation, for possible action by the Provisional World Parliament and Provisional World Government.

8. The Nominating Commission shall prepare, in advance of convening the Provisional World Parliament, a list of nominees to compose the Presidium and the Executive Cabinet for the Provisional World Government.

9. The Finance Commission shall work on ways and means for financing the Provisional World Government.

10. The several commissions on particular world problems shall work on the preparation of proposed world legislation and action on each problem, to present to the Provisional World Parliament when it convenes.

SECTION C.   COMPOSITION OF THE PROVISIONAL WORLD PARLIAMENT

1. The Provisional World Parliament shall be composed of the following members:

   a) All those who were accredited as delegates to the 1977 and 1991 Sessions of the World Constituent Assembly, as well as to any previous Session of the Provisional World Parliament, and who re-confirm their support for the Constitution for the Federation of Earth, as amended.

   b) Persons who obtain the required number of signatures on election petitions, or who are designated by Non-Governmental Organizations which adopt approved resolutions for this purpose, or who are otherwise accredited according to terms specified in Calls which may be issued to convene particular sessions of the Provisional World Parliament.

   c) Members of the World Parliament to the House of Peoples who are elected from World Electoral and Administrative Districts up to the time of convening the Provisional World Parliament. Members of the World Parliament elected to the House of Peoples may continue to be added to the Provisional World Parliament until the first operative stage of World Government is reached.

   d) Members of the World Parliament to the House of Nations who are elected by national legislatures or appointed by national governments up to the time of convening the Provisional World Parliament.

Members of the World Parliament to the House of Nations may continue to be added to the Provisional World Parliament until the first operative stage of World Government is reached.

e) Those universities and colleges which have ratified the World Constitution may nominate persons to serve as Members of the World Parliament to the House of Counsellors. The House of Peoples and House of Nations together may then elect from such nominees up to fifty Members of the World Parliament to serve in the House of Counsellors of the Provisional World Government.

2. Members of the Provisional World Parliament in categories (a) and (b) as defined above, shall serve only until the first operative stage of World Government is declared, but may be duly elected to continue as Members of the World Parliament during the first operative stage.

SECTION D. FORMATION OF THE PROVISIONAL WORLD EXECUTIVE

1. As soon as the Provisional World Parliament next convenes, it will elect a new Presidium for the Provisional World Parliament and Provisional World Government from among the nominees submitted by the Nominating Commission.

2. Members of the Provisional World Presidium shall serve terms of three years, and may be re-elected by the Provisional World Parliament, but in any case shall serve only until the Presidium is elected under the First Operative Stage of World Government.

3. The Presidium may make additional nominations for the Executive Cabinet.

4. The Provisional World Parliament shall then elect the members of the Executive Cabinet.

5. The Presidium shall then assign ministerial posts among the members of the Executive Cabinet and of the Presidium.

6. When steps (1) through (4) of section D are completed, the Provisional World Government shall be declared in operation to serve the welfare of humanity.

SECTION E. FIRST ACTIONS OF THE PROVISIONAL WORLD GOVERNMENT

1. The Presidium, in consultation with the Executive Cabinet, the commissions on particular world problems and the World Parliament, shall define a program for action on urgent world problems.

2. The Provisional World Parliament shall go to work on the agenda of world problems, and shall take any and all actions it considers

appropriate and feasible, in accordance with the provisions of this World Constitution.

3. Implementation of and compliance with the legislation enacted by the Provisional World Parliament shall be sought on a voluntary basis in return for the benefits to be realized, while strength of the Provisional World Government is being increased by the progressive ratification of the World Constitution.

4. Insofar as considered appropriate and feasible, the Provisional World Parliament and Provisional World Executive may undertake some of the actions specified under Section C-12 of Article XVII for the first operative stage of World Government.

5. The World Economic Development Organization and the World Disarmament Agency shall be established, for correlated actions.

6. The World Parliament and the Executive Cabinet of the Provisional World Government shall proceed with the organization of other organs and agencies of the World Government on a provisional basis, insofar as considered desirable and feasible, in particular those specified under Section C-10 of Article XVII.

7. The several preparatory commissions on urgent world problems may be reconstituted as Administrative Departments of the Provisional World Government.

8. In all of its work and activities, the Provisional World Government shall function in accordance with the provisions of this Constitution for the Federation of Earth.

The Constitution for the Federation of Earth was originally ratified at the second session of the World Constituent Assembly held at Innsbruck, Austria, in June, 1977; and was amended and ratified at the fourth session of the World Constituent Assembly held at Troia, Portugal, in May 1991. The Amended Constitution is being personally ratified by outstanding personalities throughout the world as the campaign for ratification by the people and governments of the world gets underway.

PARTICIPANTS IN THE WORLD CONSTITUENT ASSEMBLY, 16 TO 29 OF JUNE, 1977,
HAVE AFFIXED THEIR SIGNATURES TO THE DRAFT OF THE CONSTITUTION
FOR THE FEDERATION OF EARTH HEREWITH:

[Signatures]

India

MEXICO

EARTH, USA

Earth, USA

Hon. Legal Advisor

Canada

Sri Lanka.

Ghana.

Botswana

(Canada) Women's Universal Movement

Fed. Rep. of Germany

U.S.A.

India.

Thailand.

Australia.

Germany

Netherlands

JAPAN

Name	Country
ANDREA VON SCHLIVOY	GERMANY
Edith Barvich	Germany
Gisela Gintzel	Germany
Klaus Thakur-Schlichtmann	Germany
Ann Mische	
Gerald Mische	World, U.S.A
Dr. Ludwig C. baum	U.S.A.
Dr. Fred Karl Scheile	W. Germany
Massauer	U.S.A
Olga Jäger	Germany
Beatrice Meyers	Germany
Elisabeth Klaubauer	U.S.A.
Theo Fenchel	INNSBRUCK
Dr. Helen K. Billings	Switzerland
Magister Kirsti Balthaspi.	USA
	Finland live in México.
Robert Rosamond	United Peoples
Valorie Hagenhuber	Federation of Earth
Herbert Gröder	Austria

Name	Country
Louis R. Gomberg	U. S. A
P. C. Malhotra	India
Hildegard Heuer	Schweiz
PURAN SINGH AZAD.	(INDIA)
Dr. Miss. Geeta Shah	INDIA.
Maria Iseli	Schweiz
Kurt Kreutz	_____
Bonnie Allen	U. S. A
Rustom M. Bharucha	India.
William Bryant	USA
Jeanne C. Burrows	Us.A. World
Leo J. Murray sa (Pax Christi USA)	
Simon R Ladd	Botswana
Mrs. Renée Dangoor	United Kingdom
Mr. J. Lelaka	Botswana
Reggie Coleman	Australia
Donald L. Colman	Australia
Tilluur Giha	AUSTRIA

Name	Country
Dr. Hildegard Durfee	U.S.A.
Kira Lynne Allen	
Samar Basu	India
Robert W. Kaminski	Earth USA, Wilm Del
Hoke Thym	Holland
Yogi Shantiswaroop	India for one world
Carmel Kussman	U.S.A.
Mortimer Lifshy	U.S.A.
J. Hermann Weys	Austria
Kim Haraside	Canada
Ana Marin	P.R.
Naim Dangoor	U.K.
E. Coorn (Sri Lanka)	
	Bangalore - India
Bernadette F. Trattner	
Craig Orr White, Ph.D.	Ohio. U.S.A.
Everett Reffa	Wisc. U.S.A.
Mildred E. Parmelee	U.S.A.
Dr. (Mrs.) Kamoo Patel	Pondichery (India)
Margaret Gadge	United Kingdom

Name	Country
Bandula Sri Gunawardhana	Sri Lanka
Margaret Isely	U. S. A.
Marijen Kenya Elisabeth	Austria
[signature]	PUERTO RICO
Gregory Alexander	U.S.A.
Edward R. Leader	Puerto Rico
[signature]	India
Dorothy L. Mann Baker	U. S. A.
Carl F. Cattaui	Earth !
morgenhauerenerig	Denmark
Heather Isely	U. S. A.
Foster Parmelee	U. S. A.
Ogola Justus	Kenya
H. A. Haensing	W. Germany
Kemper Isely	U.S.A.
Bernard Shaw Magi	Nigeria
Mitsuo Miyake	JAPAN
Johanna Materhell	Netherlands
[signature]	Botswana

Name   *Address*

Eggert, Charlotte Luise   Deutschland

Josphine Baker   N.Y. C. USA

Martha Fillebun   USA

Paternolli Kurt   Innsbrück Austria

Suzanne Gomberg   San Francisco USA

Holzapfel Heiner   Innsbruck

Holzapfel Amalie   Innsbruck

Veera C. Herold   Mexico Unity

Huvel Ingeborg   Germany

Schmeding, Hans-Friedrich   Germany

Wary, Ludwig   Germany

B. Molcar   World Citizen

Leland P. Stewart   Los Angeles

John Stockwell   San Francisco

Guido Graziani   Rome, Italy

Dorothea Sarban   Hannover, WOMAN

Name   Country

[signature] Holla

[signature] iren

[signature] U.S.A.

Carmel Painter U S A

Janet Self USA

Stephen Sophie *[signature]*

[signatures] Pakistan

[signature] Bruno *[signature]* Italy México

Por el mundo espiritual
[signature] Dr. Jose M. *[signature]*

Por la unión en el arte en el espíritu (México)
Sra. Elsa *[signature]*

Rev. GAGPA Maria Carlota *[signature]* Estrada (México)

"Por el mundo Espiritual"
Rev. GagPa *[signature]* (México)

"Por el mundo Espiritual
W. Resp. 6ptals. Adolfo Olivera *[signature]* (méxico)

Name	Country
Tiakogee Ruge	Mexico
Stefanie Gollinger	Austria
[illegible]	Austria
Herbert [illegible]	Deutschland (BRD)
Siddhartha I. Patel	Kenya.
Kalaben Patel.	India
Umesh A Patel	Great Britain.
Kumud I. Patel	Great Britain.
Ahmad Subanjo S.	Indonesia
Asetyobudiarti	Indonesia
Sybil Sticht	New Zealand + USA
Alice Stephens	England.
Elizabeth E. Stewart	United States
[illegible]	Bangladesh
HARBHAJAN SINGH Khalsa Yogiji Sikh Dharma Western Hemisphere	USA

Note: This list of initial signers of the CONSTITUTION FOR THE FEDERATION OF EARTH would include several hundred more persons from fifty countries, prevented only by the cost of travel to attend the Assembly at Innsbruck, Austria.

PERSONAL RATIFIERS OF THE CONSTITUTION FOR THE FEDERATION OF EARTH AS AMENDED AT THE 4TH SESSION OF THE WORLD CONSTITUENT ASSEMBLY HELD AT TROIA, PORTUGAL, 29TH APRIL TO 9TH MAY, 1991

Prof. Dr. Kalman Abraham, Hungary

Atiku Abubakar, Nigeria

Dr. Ebenezer Ade. Adenekan, Nigeria

Malcolm S. Adiseshiah, India

Abdur Rahim Ahamed, Bangladesh

Shahzada Kabir Ahmed

Mohsin A. Alaini, Yemen

MD. Nural Alam, U.S.A.

MD. Maser Ali, Bangladesh

Dr. Terence P. Amerasinghe, Sri Lanka

Samir Amin, Senegal

Benjamin K. Amonoo, Ghana

George Anca, Romania

Mauricio Andres-Ribeiro, Brazil

Dr. Munawar A. Anees, U.S.A.

Rev. Ebenezer Annan, Ivory Coast

Jose Ayala-Lasso, Ecuador

Ir. Hasan Basri, Indonesia

Samar Basu, India

Tony Benn, United Kingdom

Prof. Mrs. Edvige Bestazzi, Italy

Petter Jakob Bjerve, Norway

Goran von Bonsdorff, Finland

Selma Brackman, U.S.A.

Jean-Marie Breton, Int. Regis. World Citizens

Tomas Bruckman, Germany (East)

Dennis Brutus, South Africa (U.S.A.)

Dr. Mihai Titus Carapancea, Romania

Prof. Henri Cartan, France

Amb. Khub Chand, India

Dr. Sripati Chandrasekhar, India

Most Rev. French Chang-Him, Seychelles

Munyaradzi Chiwashira, Zimbabwe

Dr. Pratap Chandra Chunder, India

Prof. Dr. Rodney Daniel, France

Daniel G. De Culla, Spain

Dr. Dimitrios J. Delivanis, Greece

Prof. Dr. Francis Dessart, Belgium

Raymond F. Douw, Germany

Prof. Hans-Peter Duerr, Germany

Kennedy Emekan, Nigeria

M. Necati Munir Ertekun, Cyprus

Douglas Nixon Everingham, Australia

John R. Ewbank, U.S.A.

Marjorie Ewbank, U.S.A.

Miss Lianmangi Fanai, India

Dr. Mark Farber, U.S.A.

Feng Ping-Chung, China

Prof. Dr. Mihnea Georghiu, Romania

Lucile W. Green, U.S.A.

Dr. Dauji Gupta, India

Kisholoy Gupta, India

Takeshi Haruki, Japan

Dr. Gerhard Herzberg, Canada

Jozsef Holp, Hungary

A. K. Fazlul Hogue, Bangladesh

Chowdhury Anwar Husain, Bangladesh

Margaret Isely, U.S.A. (Earth)

Philip Isely, U.S.A. (Earth)

Ram K. Jiwanmitra, Nepal

Roy E. Johnstone, Jamaica

Mohammed Kamaluddin, Bangladesh

Mohammad Rezaul Karim, Bangladesh

Rev. George Karunakeran, India

Dr. Inamullah Khan, Pakistan

Johnson S. Khan, Pakistan

Roger Kotila, Ph.D., U.S.A.

David M. Krieger, U.S.A.

Diemuth Kuebart, Germany

Jul Lag, Norway

Ben M. Leito, Netherlands Antilles

Thomas Lim, East Malaysia

Adam Lopatka, Poland

Anwarul Majid, Bangladesh

·Dr. M. Sadiq Malik, Pakistan

Guy Marchand, France

Alvin M. Marks, U.S.A.

Bernardshaw Mazi, Nigeria

Dr. Zhores A. Medvedev, U. K. (USSR)

Anna Medvegey, Hungary

R. C. Mehrotra, India

Charles Mercieca, U.S.A.

Lt. Col. Pedro B. Merida, Philippines

Yerucham Meshel, Israel

Sheta Mikayele, Zaire

Mohamed Ezzedine Mili, Switzerland

Rev. Toshic Miyake, Japan

Shettima Ali Monguno, Nigeria

Swapan Mukherjee, India

Hanna Newcombe, Canada

Brij P. Nigam, India

Josephine Okafor, Nigeria

Johnson Olatunde, Sierre Leone

Rev. Nelson Onono-Onweng, Uganda

Umit Ozturk, Turkey

Yasar Ozturk, Turkey

Linus Pauling, U.S.A.

Fernando Perez Tella, Spain

Emil Otto Peter, Austria

Dr. Alex Quaison-Sackey, Ghana

Soili Raikkonen, Finland

Sudhir Kumar Rangh, India

Thane Read, U.S.A.

Dr. Sayed Qassem Reshtia, Switzerland

Erzebet Rethy, Hungary

Miguel B. Ricardo, Portugal

G. Rivas Mijares, Venezuela

Reinhart Ruge, Mexico

Prof. Sir A. M. Sadek, South Africa

Abdus Salam, Italy

Akbar Ali Saleh, Comoros Islands

Blagovest Sendov, Bulgaria

Indira Shrestha, Nepal

Rabi Charan Shrestha, Nepal

Jon Silkin, United Kingdom

Jozef Simuth, Slovak Republic

Dr. Kewal Singh, India

Blaine Sloan, U.S.A.

Ross Smyth, Canada

Lord Donald Soper, United Kingdom

Scott Jefferson Starquester, U.S.A.

Homi J. H. Taleyarkhan, India

Rev. Yoshiaki Toeda, Japan

Dr. Duja K. Torki, Tunisia

Helen Tucker, Canada

Evelyn Utulu, Nigeria

Mrs. Justina N. Uwechue, Nigeria

Ogieva O. Uwuigbe, Nigeria

Ann Valentin, U.S.A.

T. Nejat Veziroglu, U.S.A.

Jorgen Laursen Vig, Denmark

George Wald, U.S.A.

Prof. D. A. Walker, United Kingdom

Richard W. Wilbur, U.S.A.

Zawadzki Sylwester, Poland

High Wray, Great Britain

Additional Original Ratifiers:

Kenneth B. Clark, U.S.A.

David Daube, U.S.A.

Nzo Ekangaki, Cameroon

DIAGRAM OF WORLD GOVERNMENT under the CONSTITUTION FOR THE FEDERATION OF EARTH

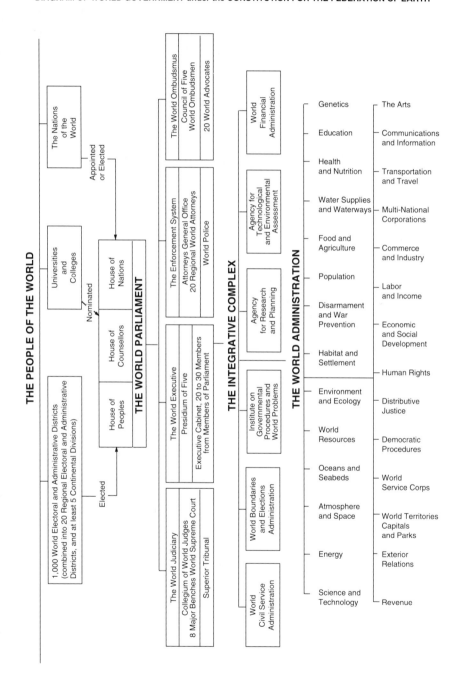

Bibliography

Agar, H., Aydelotte, F., Borgese, G. A., Broch, H., Brooks, van W., Comstock, A. L., Elliott, W. Y., Fisher, D. C., Gauss, C., Jaszi, O., Johnson, A., Kohn, H., Mann, T., Mumford, L., Neilson, W. A., Niebuhr, R., and Salvemini, G. *The City of Man*. New York: Viking Press, 1940.

Barker, E. *Principles of Social and Political Theory*. Oxford: Clarendon Press, 1951.

Bassett, Noble P. *Constitution of the United Nations of the World*. Boston, MA: Christopher Publishing House, 1944.

———. *Federation of the World*. San Francisco, CA: Murdock Press, 1906.

Borgese, G. A. *Foundations of the World Republic*. Chicago, IL: Chicago University Press, 1953.

Breitner, T. C. *World Constitution: A Study on the Legal Framework of a World Federation*. Berkeley, CA: 1963.

Brown, L. A., ed. *State of the World*. Annual Worldwatch Report. New York: W. W. Norton and Co., 1992.

Carr, E. H. *The Twenty Year Crisis*. London: Macmillan, 1939–81.

Clark, G., and Sohn, L. B. *Peace through Law*. Chapel Hill, NC: University of North Carolina Press, 1944.

Collingwood, R. G. *The New Leviathan*. Oxford: Clarendon Press, 1942.

Crozier, A. O. *Nation of Nations: The Way to Permanent Peace: A Supreme Constitution for the Government of Governments*. Cincinnati, OH: Stewart and Kidd Co., 1915.

Curry, W. B. *The Case for Federal Union*. Harmondsworth, England: Penguin Books, 1939.

Curtis, L. *Civitas Dei*. London: G. Allen and Unwin, 1938.

———. *The Way to Peace*. London: Oxford University Press, 1941.

———. *World War, Its Cause and Cure*. London: Oxford University Press, 1945.

Duguit, L. *Traité du droit constitutionnel*. Paris: Boccard, 1921.

Falk, R. *Explorations at the Edge of Time: The Prospects for World Order*. Philadelphia, PA: Temple University Press, 1992.

Ferencz, B. B., and Keyes, K. *Planethood*. Coos Bay, OR: Vision Books, 1988.

Gore, A. *The Earth in the Balance: Ecology and the Human Spirit*. Boston, New York, and London: Houghton Mifflin, 1992.

Green, T. H. *Lectures on Political Obligation*. London: Longmans, 1924.

Hamilton, A., Jay, J., and Madison, J. *The Federalist*. Washington, DC: National Home Library; New York: Random House, 1938.

197

Hammond, A., ed. *The 1992 Environmental Almanac.* Compiled by World Resources Institute. Boston, MA: Houghton Mifflin, 1992.

Harris, E. E. *Annihilation and Utopia.* London: G. Allen and Unwin, 1966.

———. *Cosmos and Anthropos.* Atlantic Highlands, NJ: Humanities Press, 1991.

———. *Cosmos and Theos.* Atlantic Highlands, NJ: Humanities Press, 1992.

———. *The Survival of Political Man.* Johannesburg: Witwatersrand University Press, 1950.

Harris, J. M. *World Agriculture and the Environment.* New York and London: Garland Publishing, Inc., 1990.

Hegel, G. W. F. *Grundlinien der Philosophie des Rechts.* Translated by T. M. Knox as *Hegel's Philosophy of Right.* Oxford: Clarendon Press, 1942–53.

Hobbes, T. *Leviathan.* Reprint of 1651 edition. Oxford: Clarendon Press, 1909, 1929–43.

Hoyland, J. S. *The World in Union.* London: Peace Book Co., 1940.

Hutchins, R. M. *Preliminary Draft of a World Constitution.* Chicago, IL: University of Chicago Press, 1948.

Jessup, P. C. *A Modern Law of Nations.* New York: Macmillan, 1952.

Johnson, J. E. *Federal World Government.* New York: Wilson and Co., 1948.

Junger, E. *Der Weltstaat, Organismus und Organisation.* Stuttgart: Klett, 1960.

Keeton, G. W. *National Sovereignty and International Order.* London: Peace Book Co., 1939.

Keeton, G. W., and Schwarzenberger, G. *Making International Law Work.* London: Peace Book Co., 1939.

Kelsen, H. *General Theory of Law and the State.* Cambridge, MA: Harvard University Press, 1945, 1949; New York: Russell and Russell, 1961.

———. *Law and Peace in International Relations.* Cambridge, MA: Harvard University Press, 1942.

Krabbe, H. *The Modern Theory of the State.* New York and London: D. Appleton and Co., 1922.

Laski, H. J. *A Grammar of Politics.* London: G. Allen and Unwin, 1926–41.

Lauterpacht, H. *The Function of Law in the International Community.* Oxford: Clarendon Press, 1933.

———. *Private Law Sources and Analogies of International Law.* New York and London: Longmans Green, 1927.

Lilienthal, A. M. *Which Way to World Government?* New York: Foreign Policy Association, 1950.

Lipsky, M. *Never Again War: The Case for World Government.* South Brunswick: A. S. Barnes, 1971.

Lothian, P. H. K., Lord. *The Ending of Armageddon.* Oxford: Aldon Press, 1939.

Lovelock, J. E. *Gaia: A New Look at Life on Earth.* New York and Oxford: Oxford University Press, 1979, 1987.

Millard, E. L. *Freedom in a Federal World.* Dobbs Ferry, NY: Oceania Publications, 1959, 1964.

Morgenthau, H. *Politics among the Nations.* New York: Knopf, 1948–78.

Newfang, O. *The Road to Peace: A Federation of the Nations.* New York and London: G. P. Putnam, 1924.

———. *World Federation.* New York: Barnes and Noble, 1939.

———. *World Government.* New York: Barnes and Noble, 1942.

Perry, R. B. *One World in the Making.* New York: Current Books, 1945.

Pinheiro, de V. H. *The World State, or the New Order of Common Sense.* Rio de Janiero: Grafica Olimpia, 1944.

Reves, E. *An Anatomy of Peace.* New York: Harper Bros., 1945; London: G. Allen and Unwin, 1946.

Robbins, L. *Economic Aspects of Federation.* London: Macmillan, 1941.

Scelle, G. *Précis de droit des gens.* 2 vols. Paris: Librarie du Recueil, 1932–34.

Schiffer, W. *The Legal Community of Mankind: A Critical Analysis of the Concept of World Organization.* New York: Columbia University Press, 1954.

Schwarzenberger, G. *Power Politics.* 2nd edition. London: Stevens and Sons Ltd., 1951.

Selander, J. B. *World Union Now.* Berkeley, CA: Gazette Press, 1944.

Spinoza, B. de. *Political Works.* Translated by A. G. Wernham. Oxford: Clarendon Press, 1958–65.

Streit, C. *Union Now, A Proposal for an Atlantic Federal Union of the Free.* New York: Harper, 1949.

———. *World Government or Anarchy? Our Urgent Need for World Order.* Chicago, IL: World Citizens Association, 1939.

Thomas, L. *The Lives of a Cell.* New York: Viking Press, 1974; Harmondsworth, England: Penguin Books, 1987.

United Nations. *World Urbanization Prospects.* New York: UN Publications, 1991.

Wagar, W. *The City of Man.* Boston, MA: Houghton Mifflin, 1963.

Wheare, K. C. *Federal Government.* London: Oxford University Press, 1946.

Wofford, H. *It's Up to Us: Federal World Government in Our Time.* New York: Harcourt Brace, 1946.

Wootton, B. *Socialism and Federation.* London: Macmillan, 1941.

World Resources Institute. *The 1992 Environmental Almanac.* Boston, MA: Houghton Mifflin, 1992.

Worldwatch. *State of the World—1992.* London: W. W. Norton and Co., 1992.

Wynner, E. *World Federal Government: Why? What? How?* Afton, NY: Fedonat Press, 1954.

Index

201